D0076871

Governing the Press

About the Book and Author

Jealously guarded and frequently defended, the concept of freedom of the press is still subject to widely varying interpretations in different democratic systems. This book compares and contrasts the ways in which the system limits and defines press freedom in two nations known for an unfettered press--the United States and Great Britain. Examining two recent and critically important case studies--the Iranian hostage crisis and the British-Argentine intervention in the Falkland Islands--the author dramatically illustrates the interaction between government and press in the United States and Great Britain. The strength of this book lies in the wealth of personal interviews with high-level government officials and journalists who were directly involved in managing and reporting the two crises. Those interviewed include Cyrus Vance, former U.S. Secretary of State; Zbigniew Brzezinski, former U.S. National Security Adviser; Sir John Nott, former British Secretary of Defence; Bernard Ingham, current Press Secretary to the Prime Minister; James Reston, Tom Wicker, and Drew Middleton, *New York Times* columnists; and John Witherow, London *Times* reporter with the Falklands task force. Through these interviews and close analysis of other primary sources, the author illuminates the conflicting goals and differences of opinion between government and press that become most distinct in times of national crisis.

Deborah Holmes, a recent graduate of Harvard University, is currently a J.D. candidate at Harvard Law School.

Governing the Press

Media Freedom in the U.S. and Great Britain

Deborah Holmes

Westview Press / Boulder and London

WIDENER UNIVERSITY
WOLFGRAM
LIBRARY
CHESTER, PA

DISCARDED
WIDENER UNIVERSITY

A Westview Special Study

This Westview softcover edition was manufactured on our own premises using
equipment and methods that allow us to keep even specialized books in
stock. It is printed on acid-free paper and bound in softcovers that
carry the highest rating of the National Association of State Textbook
Administrators, in consultation with the Association of American Publishers
and the Book Manufacturers' Institute.

All rights reserved. No part of this publication may be reproduced or
transmitted in any form or by any means, electronic or mechanical,
including photocopy, recording, or any information storage and retrieval
system, without permission in writing from the publisher.

Copyright © 1986 by Westview Press, Inc.

Published in 1986 in the United States of America by Westview Press, Inc.;
Frederick A. Praeger, Publisher; 5500 Central Avenue, Boulder, Colorado
80301

Library of Congress Cataloging-in-Publication Data
Holmes, Deborah.
    Governing the press.
    (Westview special study)
    Bibliography: p.
    Includes index.
    1. Government and the press--Great Britain.
2. Freedom of the press--Great Britain. 3. Falkland
Islands War, 1982--Journalists. 4. Government and
the press--United States. 5. Freedom of the press--
United States. 6. Iran Hostage Crisis, 1979-1981.
I. Title. II. Series: Westview special studies.
PN4748.G7H64 1986   302.2'34'0941   86-7784
ISBN 0-8133-7196-1

Composition for this book was provided by the author.
This book was produced without formal editing by the publisher.

Printed and bound in the United States of America

The paper used in this publication meets the minimum requirements of the American National Standard for Permanence of
Paper for Printed Library Materials Z39.48-1984.

6   5   4   3   2   1

For my parents,
Monica Bychowski Holmes and Douglas Holmes,
without whom this book
— among other things —
would never have happened.

Contents

Acknowledgments

I accept full responsibility for the theories and arguments presented in this book. Nevertheless, I would like to take this opportunity to express my gratitude to all those who helped.

For their generosity in contributing their time and observations, I would like to thank everyone I interviewed who was involved in managing or reporting the two crises that constitute the focus of this book: Stuart Auerbach, Anthony Barnett, Zbigniew Brzezinski, Edward Cody, Dave Gergen, Tony Holden, Bernard Ingham, Henry James, Ian McDonald, Drew Middleton, John Nott, Jody Powell, James Reston, Hal Saunders, Elaine Sciolino, John Underwood, Cyrus Vance, Tom Wicker and John Witherow.

For his careful readings and advice, I want to thank my thesis adviser, Hugh Heclo, Professor of Government at Harvard University.

For bringing to this book all the experience of an Englishman – not to mention the wisdom of a don at both Oxford and Cambridge – I thank Simon Schama, Professor of History at Harvard University.

For their patience, humor and encouragement, I wish to thank Joe Garcia and Monique Richards, who helped me to make much of our four years as Harvard undergraduates.

And – even though he had no effect at all on this book – for having the right interests, I thank Andrew Arends.

Deborah Holmes

1

The Press in Britain
and the United States

Both in the United States and in Britain, newspapers are subject to economic and political pressures. As will be seen below through analysis of these pressures and of various responses to them, the press in the two countries are radically dissimilar. Legal institutions and cultural expectations have made the media incomparably more powerful in the United States than in Britain. Closer relations with government officials and greater liberty to print controversial information have entrenched the American press in a position of power which is rarely questioned. In England, the press is hampered by restrictive legislation and mores.

A FREE PRESS

More than other institutions, the media of every nation are shaped largely by the type of political power that prevails in the country. Most organizations are bound only to observe the law of the land; the press is unique because it publicizes the rules by which it plays. In authoritarian states this publicity translates into pro-government propaganda. In democratic countries, the publicity function of the press serves to inform the voting public about the actions of officials. In both cases the press is intimately involved with the process of governing, and as a result it "takes on the form and coloration of the social and political structures within which it operates."[1] Whether public relations officer, as in authoritarian regimes, or self-appointed watchdog, as in democratic countries, the press thrives on government. Living cheek by jowl with the organs of national power, the press is influenced by the political and social culture within which it operates.

1

In the United States and England, this cultural influence is exerted in favor of a free press. During the eighteenth century the press acquired the right to publish information critical of government; during the early years of the twentieth century the notion of objective journalism began to supplant editorialized reporting as newspapers with diametrically opposed editorial policies began subscribing to wire services, which supplied facts without the accompanying interpretations which inevitably would offend some client. Belief in objective reporting as the proper form for journalism was strengthened after World War Two, when previously ironclad beliefs were shattered by the experience of atrocities without known precedent in the western world. Objective reporting, then, has become the accepted mode of describing events.

The goal of political objectivity — which, attainable or not, remains the lodestar of most journalists — has an economic counterpart in newspapers' efforts to remain financially independent. In theory it should be possible for the government to protect the media from the undirected operation of the free market, which does not permit the existence of a well-balanced, fully representative press.

In actual fact the government almost never intervenes in the market on behalf of the press; at most, a newspaper might accept a small financial concession from the state. In Britain the press is exempt from taxing sales and advertising, and consequently enjoys a fiscal advantage worth five to ten percent of total revenue.[2] However, even this relatively minor tax exemption is regarded with extreme suspicion by English journalists. Independent Television News reporter John Underwood, for example, believes that the British press purchases economic assistance at the price of dependence on government, and therefore is highly susceptible to state censorship. The alternative — economic freedom from government, which necessitates total reliance on advertising revenues — appeals to Underwood no more strongly. "Basically, it's the devil or the deep blue sea," he says.[3]

Unfortunately, unswerving opposition to government funding ignores the fact that the pure market creates other, equally imperative forms of pressure and distortion. Competition from alternative news sources, technological constraints, and the need to woo advertisers all pose serious problems for the press in Britain and the United States.

Alternative sources of news — television, radio, weekly magazines and other periodicals — constitute the greatest danger to newspapers. The closure of papers is particularly significant in the United States, where cities which previously supported a wide range of titles have become one-newspaper towns.[4] In Britain, by contrast, newspapers are organized nationally, so even at the zenith of newspaper popularity few cities boasted more than a single local daily. As a result, the recent closures have affected the country as a whole rather than specific localities.

The need to modernize poses an additional problem for newspapers. In both the United states and Britain, obsolete technology and overmanning contribute to high production costs even as increasing suburbanization requires investment in expensive delivery systems. However, the localization of the American press gives it an enormous advantage. The vast size of the United States, and the subsequent difficulty of appealing with national titles to its heterogeneous population, has ensured that small towns rarely support more than one title. Even in cities newspapers have specialized their appeal in order to attract, unchallenged, a single discrete market. When new cost-saving technology became available, therefore, American newspapers could afford to halt publication while they modernized. "As none of these papers were subject to serious local competition, they could be suspended in the secure knowledge that their market would be waiting for them when they returned."[5]

In Britain, by contrast, a compact population supporting a nationally subsidized railway network permits easy distribution of "a multiplicity of titles available nationwide [which] is unequalled in any other Western country."[6] However, the national organization of the English press subjects the major newspapers to intense competition in all localities, and therefore prevented Fleet Street titles from risking the temporary closures necessary to install new technology.

Financially threatened by alternative news sources, and often unable to afford technological modernization, newspapers increasingly are forced to depend on advertising revenues to supplement declining sales. In England, sales constitute only 39 percent of the total budget of the quality press, with the remaining 60 percent coming from advertising, while the popular press can rely on sales to comprise 72 percent of its budget, with advertisements supplying the remainder.[7] In America newspapers count even more heavily on advertising.[8]

The efforts of newspaper publishers to survive in the free market may have untoward consequences. Recently the press in Britain and the United States have been accused of standardizing editorial policies and of deepening the class differences that divide society. To some extent, these allegations are justified.

In the United States, newspapers with liberal leanings are most highly respected — journalists and politicians of all political stripes rely on the <u>New York Times</u> and the <u>Washington Post</u>[9] — while in England conservatism prevails. Of Britain's eight national dailies, only two are not conservative, and even these are barely distinguishable from their supposedly less liberal competitors on the Right.

> The right-wing popular papers are, in general, on the right wing of Conservative opinion, while the <u>Mirror,</u> supposed to be the countervailing force, is, again in general, on the right wing of Labour opinion.[10]

In both the American and the British press, then, a definite overall bias can be detected.

The skew in the American and British press can be explained in terms of their tendency to adjust to market forces. One excellent technique for outmaneuvering the market is the formation of newspaper monopolies, whereby a single publisher owns numerous titles. Usually, such monopolies are created not in order to homogenize editorial content but in the hopes of making a career in newspaper publishing financially viable.[11] However, as the case of Rupert Murdoch amply illustrates, it is possible for concentrated ownership to influence the general character and political slant of the press in a country. In the United States this influence has been exerted in favor of liberal editorial policies; in Britain, the reverse situation has obtained.

One reason for the fact that the market tends to favor editorial conservatism in Britain and not in the United States is the national orientation of the English press. Newspapers in the United Kingdom are far more competitive than in America, where every title serves a distinct geographical market. Because papers compete not only for readers but also for advertisers, publishers are biased in favor of readers whose high potential buying power attracts advertisers.

> Newspapers are among the few products for which one buyer's money is not as good as another's in the eyes of the seller: 8p a day from a reader earning £5000 a year is worth much more than 8p from a reader earning £2000 a year, because a newspaper is not just selling its editorial policy to its readers but is selling the readers' income to advertisers.[12]

As a result, publishers prefer to produce newspapers which appeal to wealthier portions of society, and neglect groups with less pull on advertisers. The consequence may be a slight general skew in the press toward monied, propertied sectors, which traditionally are politically conservative. As competition is fiercer in Britain than in the United States, so too may be this skew, manifested in editorial conservatism.

If it is likely that market forces affect the editorial policy of newspapers, it is virtually certain that these forces influence the social orientation of the press. Newspapers must fit into existing niches of political opinion, and extensive market research indicates that these niches are closely correlated with social class.[13] In Britain, the press is polarized between popular and quality titles, and the appearance of diversity fostered by the existence of numerous national daily newspapers is misleading. Each title claims a distinct social group as its readership, "and competes with other papers only at the fringes of its circulation."[14] In the United States, because of the absence of national newspapers and the tendency toward regional monopoly, class divisions in newspaper readership are plainly demarcated only in large cities which support more than one title. In both countries, however, quality newspapers are read by the middle and upper classes, while tabloids cater to the lower classes. In other words, the need to capture some market prompts newspapers to perpetuate the values and prejudices that characterize their readers' social class.

NATIONAL SECURITY

Even the most doggedly libertarian theorists admit to the existence of some restrictions on freedom of the press. For the most part these restrictions take the form of anti-defamation laws designed to protect individual reputations. In addition, many countries have legal injunctions against the publication of materials that may endanger the integrity of the state. Even in the absence of specific legislation, the principle of secrecy is widely accepted in all countries. As James Reston writes in The Artillery of the Press, "In this time of half-war and half-peace the principle of publish-and-be-damned, while very romantic, bold and hairy, can often damage the national interest."[15] Thus journalists admit the necessity of exercising self-restraint in order to avoid endangering the security interests of their country.

Journalistic Self-Restraint

Indeed, to a degree that confounds general assumptions about
the devil-may-care attitude of the press, newspapers in both
Britain and the United States are willing to engage in self-
restraint on the recommendation of government officials. In
On Press, Tom Wicker writes that

> There seems to be a public impression that the
> press leaps at any chance to rush into print with
> government secrets, scarcely pausing to think
> about, or happily ignoring, the consequences. If
> so, few impressions are more erroneous. Neither
> does the press leap at such chances nor does it
> brush off the possible consequences.[16]

In fact, newspapers may be overly well-intentioned toward
government.

> The press may be overeager to demonstrate its
> responsibility at the expense of its independence
> and its judgment...the track record of American
> news organizations in suppressing material when the
> government has taken the press into its confidence
> is good, perhaps too good....the press keeps both
> diplomatic and military secrets when asked to do
> so.[17]

The reasons for this cooperative spirit are two. First,
the state enjoys the enormous advantage of power over
newspapers. Fear of recrimination prompts many journalists
to refrain from repeating stories which the government does
not want told. In both America and the United Kingdom,
the state has shown itself ready to issue subpoenas to the
press, and government lawsuits take a heavy toll on
newspaper finances and reputation. Less extreme than a
lawsuit, but no less damaging to the press, is the state's
ability to punish non-cooperative reporters or newspapers by
severing contact temporarily. A journalist whose telephone
calls to government officials are not returned, and who loses
valuable sources to rivals on other newspapers, often regrets
the initial decision to report a contested story.
A second reason for the willingness of the press to
honor government requests in both Britain and the United
States is the reluctance of journalists to destroy the aura of
conspiratorial conviviality that often prevails at press
briefings. According to Wicker,

a reporter who knows something that cannot be
printed for national-security reasons is elevated
himself into that prized masculine circle of power,
knowledge, authority, responsibility. He becomes
the ultimate insider; and the reporter's deadliest
enemy — the desire to be an accepted part of the
world of power all around him — has won its final
victory.[18]

In other words, many journalists would sooner remain among
the knowledgeable elite than report the secrets they have
learned.

Government Secrecy

Nevertheless, journalistic self-restraint often does not
measure up to the standards of a close-mouthed government
bureaucracy.   Carter Administration White House press
secretary Jody Powell states,

I think it works on the whole, if you're talking
about disclosure of specific information that has a
direct and serious impact on national security, that
jeopardizes lives or blows up a whole operation.
But it doesn't work in areas that are much more
nebulous, much more gray, not calamitous....That, I
think, is one of the things that journalism lacks, is
fear of what will happen if you screw it
up....There is nothing quite like the healthy fear of
government officials who know that they are going
to be held personally responsible.[19]

In both Britain and the United States, the fear that
reporters will expose what Powell calls "gray areas" causes
material whose importance to national security is questionable
to be designated Classified. Particularly during peacetime, it
is difficult to justify the existence of numerous Classified
documents. In a 1983 interview, Tom Wicker stated,

I don't think there are more than two handfuls of
real national security secrets, and most of them
wouldn't be newsworthy... What's left that might be
of interest to some people is very closely guarded.
You're not just going to barge in and say
irresponsibly, "To hell with the national security."[20]

In other words, according to Wicker the nation possesses few genuine secrets, and these are completely inviolate.

The fact that Classified documents exist in great numbers, then, seems to reflect the personal concerns of the officials who wield the Classified stamp. Some of these officials seek only to conceal their own inefficiencies and corruption. Indeed, government personnel are "naturally tempted to paper over a personal embarrassment or a partisan disagreement with a secret classification and say they are acting in the name of national security."[21] In addition to the desire to protect personal reputations, the fear of acting irresponsibly may cause officials to wield the Classified stamp indiscriminately: low-level civil servants face higher penalties for insufficient caution than for over-zealous classification, and consequently they err on the side of safety by restricting materials of no particular importance.[22]

Great Britain. In addition to the right to designate documents as Classified, the British state has at its disposal a panoply of measures designed to protect it from the investigations of the press. The Official Secrets Act, which is largely responsible for the caution that characterizes British newspapers when addressing political issues, is divided into two parts. Section One "prohibits the passing of any information which might indirectly assist an enemy for the purpose of prejudicing the interests of the state."[23] The state defines its own interests, and the burden of proof in case of disagreement is on the press. Section Two punishes journalists who receive confidential information from government personnel. This sanction is invoked selectively, when officials attempting to conceal government inefficiency or corruption prefer not to speak with reporters or when officials wish to favor certain newspapers over others by granting access to privileged information. In addition to its potential for inconsistent application, Section Two is so wide-ranging that it can be used to exceed the bounds within which the Act was originally intended to function.

Reluctance to run afoul of either section of the Official Secrets Act fosters extreme journalistic discretion and consequently a tendency for exposes to appear only after the danger of punishment has passed. In order to aid newspapers in the exercise of caution, in 1912 the government established the D-Notice Committee, which periodically issues guidelines delineating the specific areas currently protected by the Official Secrets Act. Henry James, former spokesman for the Office of the Prime Minister, describes D-Notices as "a reminder to the journalist of his own professionalism."[24]

The United States. By contrast, the United States gained national independence against a backdrop of newspaper attacks on British colonial authorities, so the new state regarded the press as an ally. In fact, whereas in England newspapers were not permitted access to Parliamentary debates until the mid-nineteenth century, in the United States the press has been privy to the meetings of the national legislature since the First Continental Congress in 1774.[25] In England, restrictions on the press are codified by law and therefore constitute a fait accompli which only extraordinary circumstances could reverse. In the United States, the press is legally unrestricted, and any attempts to legislate limits to its freedom would require clearance by the judicial branch of government.

To date, efforts to restrict the press in America have foundered on the unwillingness of the Supreme Court to countenance encroachments on the First Amendment. The failure of attempts to induce prior restraint — the right of government to stop publication of a story before it is printed — permit the American press to "publish and be damned, because damnation comes after, and not before, publication has taken place."[26]

Even post facto damnation is rarely terrible in the United States, because the press is not legally barred from printing Classified information. Only the National Security Agency, which handles codes, is protected by law. For each of the two stipulations of the British Official Secrets Act, the United States has a contrary rule. In both countries the press is forbidden to publish Classified information relevant to national security. In the United Kingdom, Section One of the Official Secrets Act forces the press to prove that stories based on Classified information do not affect national security. In America, by contrast, the burden of proof that national security has been violated rests with the government.

> In America the onus of proof that any particular piece of secrecy is necessary lies with the person who is imposing the restriction. In Britain it is assumed that unless you can establish a clear right to know, it is better that you should not. [27]

By the same token, unlike in Britain, where Section Two of the Official Secrets Act sanctions the punishment of journalists when government secrets appear in newspapers, in the United States the culprits are the leaky officials.[28]

RELATIONS BETWEEN GOVERNMENT AND THE PRESS

The American press thus enjoys greater power and prestige than does the British press. As English journalist Anthony Holden remarks, "Reporters in America are high-status people. Reporters here are people in dirty raincoats who walk in gutters."[29] Indeed, British public servants indicate less respect for the press than do government officials in the United States. Americans generally conceive of the press as a skeptical observer of government with special rights designed to assist it in its task of informing the public. This concept is foreign to Britain, where officials deny journalists all prerogatives not held by other citizens, and describe reporters as opinionated, flagrantly non-objective, and "lazy; they don't do their homework."[30]

The Status of the Press

In both countries the interests of state and press — except when officials welcome coverage of some positive development — are often opposed, with policymakers frequently working under conditions of the maximum possible secrecy and reporters thriving on conflict and publicity. Indeed, the loftiest function of the press in democracy is to disclose government misdemeanors to the voting public, because officials are not trusted to pursue the best interests of the people. Numerous devices have been invented in democratic countries to prevent government from subverting the rights of its citizens. Not the least of these devices is the libertarian press, whose watchfulness helps keep officials in line and whose exposes of misbehavior in government initiate the process of punishing the miscreants.

Great Britain. In the United Kingdom, the watchdog function of the press is minimal, with newspapers playing a subdued role in keeping government responsible.

They serve to bring issues into focus and to make government leaders anxious and answerable for their conduct. At the same time they refrain from probing the government in such a way as to do lasting damage.[31]

Lasting damage to an individual Government, it is thought, would undermine the government in general and therefore must be avoided even at the price of permitting infractions of the law to go unreported.

Nor does the British press influence specific events or policies in government. To be sure, reporters receive regular briefings from the office of the Prime Minister, from Parliament and the Parliamentary Opposition, and from individual Members of Parliament (MPs). But these briefings almost never provide reporters with inside information which they can use in investigating delicate stories on government. For one thing, the spokesman for No. 10 Downing Street speaks only to a select, carefully chosen group of reporters, while the Prime Minister addresses the press rarely and refers to general issues rather than to specific policy decisions.[32]

Other briefings resemble bland prepared press releases, because the real business of investigating government activity is done by the government itself. As James Reston commented in a recent interview, "the Prime Minister in Britain feels obliged to report first to the Parliament."[33] Four times weekly, each time for an hour, the Question Period gives MPs in the House of Commons the opportunity to query Government ministers about recent initiatives.

The fact that the English Question Period is conducted by members of government while the American press conference is engineered by external observers constitutes a fascinating paradigm of the different roles of the press in the two countries. In Britain, newspapers take a back seat to government, and journalists function only as reporters in the strict sense of the word. In the United States, the press is integrally involved in the process of governing.

The United States. Indeed, American journalists are widely considered equally as important as government officials.

> The Washington press corps has certainly acquired the trappings of power. Privileged as no other citizens are, the correspondents are listed in the Congressional Directory; they receive advance copies of governmental speeches and announcements; they are frequently shown documents forbidden even to high officials; and they meet and work in special quarters set aside for them in all major government buildings, including the White House. Fantastic quantities of government time and money are devoted to their needs, their desires, and their whims.[34]

Not surprisingly, policymakers favor journalists for instrumental reasons. In the first place, knowledgeable reporters often furnish officials with useful information. In

the second place, the United States government is characterized by its impossibly "vast size, geographical diffuseness,
and insularity,"[35] and officials rely on the press as a sort of
in-house mail system.   By publicizing an initiative in the
press, policymakers capture the attention of other officials,
whose support may be critical to the success of the proposed
measure.   Finally, good publicity helps ambitious politicians
to advance their careers and their pet policies by winning
them favor among government officials and the voting public
alike.   Positive relations with journalists are particularly important for Congressmen, who must pull out every stop in
order to succeed in the complex, fragmented world of
Washington politics.

 Nevertheless, members of the legislative branch often
express anger at the alleged unreliability, irresponsibility and
bias of the press.[36]   All too often, reporters without full
access to the facts file incomplete stories merely to prevent
being scooped by a rival; at the same time, concern with
attracting readers prompts sensationalistic treatment of
issues.   Frequently, public officials resent journalists who
either fail to report information that would advance the interests of government or publish material despite its potential harm to national concerns.   On a more trivial level,
Congressmen do not take kindly to being ignored, so they
become miffed when journalists reporting the outcome of a
debate in Congress want only vote tallies and care nothing
for the opinions of individual politicians.   By the same
token, even though members of Congress rarely have access
to Classified information, Congressmen feel personally insulted
when they are bypassed by reporters investigating high-level
secrets.

 To some extent, relations between Congressmen and
journalists on the trail of major stories are irrelevant, because good investigative reporters generally work for important daily newspapers, and members of Congress are concerned primarily with receiving positive exposure in the local
newspapers of their constituencies.   The President, on the
other hand, needs to curry favor with a national electorate,
so he pays careful attention to his coverage in the major
titles.   Generally, the press vacillates between representing
the Chief Executive as "the leader who symbolizes our national purpose and the leader who is to be held accountable
for the acts of his lowliest subordinates."[37]   Frequently
reporters are hostile to the President, with whom they cannot establish the personal, exclusive ties that characterize
their relations with Congressmen.   Nevertheless, in his dealings with journalists the President has the upper hand simply

by virtue of being the newsmaker rather than the commentator.

The nature of interactions between reporters and the Chief Executive sets the tone for the entire administration: Presidential friendliness toward the press engenders cordiality at lower levels of government, while executive hostility toward journalists fosters similar antagonism among the rank-and-file. Of course, regardless of the example set by the President, some officials radiate confidence and ease in their dealings with the press, while others are timorous and discomfited.

Whatever the attitude of a particular administration toward the press, newspapers always have at their disposal the not inconsiderable power to put topics on the political agenda. By publicizing some issues and ignoring others, the press serves to illuminate or obscure government initiatives.

> When two or more major developments take place simultaneously, the newspaperman's view of the news is subject to strain; an obvious way to lift the strain is to reimpose the hierarchy of importance, treating one of the developments as if it were qualitatively different — more important, more interesting — than the others.[38]

Such a hierarchy serves to define for policymakers the current political universe to which they should turn their attention.

This power over the political agenda causes American reporters to hold themselves in extremely high esteem. Indeed, newspapers rarely contain analyses of events by non-reporters who are expert in the relevant field, because the opinions of editorial columnists are regarded as sufficient.[39] Most journalists perceive themselves as members of a fourth branch of government whose function and high status are crucial to the health of society. "The press likes to see itself as an agent for change, reforming and crusading."[40] As a result, "the reporter's view that he is performing a sacred calling can cloak him with an annoying self-righteousness about his mission."[41]

Information Dissemination by Government

Self-importance notwithstanding, no journalist is better than his information, so the process of acquiring news is important in both Britain and the United States. Government officials communicate with the press in four basic ways. Reports issued on the record may be quoted and attributed to the politician who delivers them, while background information may be quoted but not attributed to a specific individual. Deep background intelligence is neither quotable nor attributable, and statements made off the record cannot be used except as personal, private verification of information gained elsewhere. Any of these four styles of issuing statements may be used either to inform all the reporters covering a specific topic or to communicate personally with a few favored journalists. However, officials who talk off the record to a large number of reporters must expect publicity as the result, because, as James Reston writes, "talking off the record to a thousand people in the United States is like making love in Grand Central Station."[42]

In fact, more often than not, officials who give off-the-record briefings to a thousand reporters are attempting deliberately to gain publicity for the topic discussed without seeming to do so. Because it provides information to the public, the press is used frequently to convey a certain message or image that cannot be transmitted deliberately for fear of blowing somebody's cover. The burgeoning size and increasing complexity of government make it impossible for journalists to detect every instance of attempted manipulation by officials.

> In the age of the nuclear warhead, the computer, the data bank, and the wiretapper, the power of the government to control information, to conceal truth, and to shape information to fit government policy has reached unprecedented levels.[43]

Susan Page, Washington correspondent for Newsday, states ruefully, "Day in, day out, the press gets used, and the big battle is, you try not to be used."[44]

News management is deployed for a number of reasons. When tricky diplomatic negotiations are in progress, officials use the press to impart views which the administration does not want to convey formally.[45]   Policymakers are hesitant to associate their names with an initiative until they are certain of its success; by pretending that the proposed policy is highly confidential, they guarantee its immediate publicity by susceptible reporters who honor the conventions of journalism to the extent that they refrain from naming their sources. Another reason for news management, particularly in the United States, is officials' desire to enhance their own prestige. "The American politician has always been something of a dramatist in search of an audience, more flamboyant, a greater individualist than his European counterpart."[46] Policymakers often use the press to enhance their own personal reputations as well as to test the waters for government initiatives. Then, too, news management may be undertaken by officials attempting to conceal blunders.

CONCLUSION

Both in Britain and the United States, then, officials can display unwillingness to cooperate with journalists and readiness to manage the news to their own liking. However, the extent and even the nature of government obscurantism and manipulation differ widely in the two countries. In America information is suppressed less frequently than in Britain, where the state's desire for secrecy is backed by legislation prohibiting publication of a wide range of materials. On the other hand, the United States government solicits the cooperation of the press and engages in news management with greater frequency than does the British state.

In other words, in England the government tends to suppress information directly, while in America officials rely largely on news management and on self-restraint by journalists. This difference of approach results not only from the greater legal power at the disposal of the British state in its dealings with the press but also from the dissimilar heritages of the two countries. The American system regards government as no more than the repository of power delegated from the people, and consequently is ideologically reluctant to hamper any institution likely to increase the efficacy of government by the informed consent of the governed. In Britain, by contrast, the state is grounded in a concept of sovereignty which originally involved the divine right of kings and therefore does not emphasize the role of the voting public, much less of the press which serves to inform it. In the United States, government and the press grew up together, so the state had no opportunity to develop secretive attitudes and national institutions. As a result, current American administrations find themselves hounded by journalists who are deeply committed to their role as watchdog of government. English journalists, by contrast, take a back seat to the state, which established its Empire and accustomed itself to power long before the emergence of Fleet Street. Not regarding the press as its equal either in

might or in importance, the British state is disinclined to enlist journalists' cooperation in handling sensitive material.
Officials in the United States, on the other hand, generally
consider the press sufficiently powerful to be worthy of
courting and, indeed, too powerful to be ignored.

The American press thus occupies a position of far
greater prestige and influence in its dealings with government
than does its British counterpart. At the same time,
newspapers in the United States are less subject than
newspapers in the United Kingdom to distorting economic
pressures. The national character of the British press subjects the country's major titles to intense competition for
both readers and advertisers in all localities. The attempt
to acquire a wealthy audience and thus high advertising
revenues in a hotly competitive market fosters editorial
conservatism. By the same token, the desire to avoid
rivalry with other titles prompts each newspaper to establish for itself a loyal readership which is socially and politically distinct from the clientele of every other newspaper. In
the United States, titles establish regional monopolies which
free them to a considerable extent from the need to address
the particular political proclivities and economic characteris-
tics of their readers.

In contrast to American newspapers, then, the British
press is restricted by legislation, slighted by tradition and
distorted by competition. All too often, this unhappy combination produces an irresponsible sensationalism which is
tempered only by journalists' eagerness to follow government
initiatives in order to gain the favor of close-mouthed
officials. In the United States, the press is secure in its
relations with government and in its regional near-monopolies
on readership. As a result, officials' requests for secrecy
rarely are honored on faith; self-restraint occurs fairly
frequently but only after careful consideration by the journalists or editors involved.

1. Fred S. Siebert, "The Libertarian Theory of the Press," in Four Theories of the Press, eds. Fred S. Siebert, Theodore Peterson, and Wilbur Schramm (Freeport NY: Books for Libraries Press, 1956), p 1.

2. Anthony Smith, "State Intervention and the Management of the Press," in The British Press: A Manifesto, ed. James Curran (London: The MacMillan Press Ltd, 1978), p 71.

3. John Underwood, Independent Television News, London, England. Interview with the author, 6 September 1983.

4. For a discussion of the economic difficulties faced by newspapers in both Britain and the United States, see Simon Jenkins, Newspapers (London: Faber and Faber, 1979), pp 74–85.

5. Ibid., p 76.

6. Ibid., p 74.

7. Harry Henry, "The Pattern of Press Revenues" in Behind the Headlines — the Business of the British Press, ed. Harry Henry (London: Associated Business Press, 1978), pp 12–15.

8. Data of comparable specificity are not available for the United States; for a general discussion of the relative importance of advertising revenues in Britain and America, see Bill Grundy, The Press Inside Out (London: W.H. Allen, 1976), p 145.

9. Rivers, The Other Government, p 219.

10. Raymond Williams, "The Press We Don't Deserve" in The British Press: A Manifesto, p 21.

11. Anthony Smith, Goodbye Gutenberg: The Newspaper Revolution of the 1980's (New York: Oxford University Press, 1980), p 55.

12. Hirsch and Gordon, Newspaper Money, p 40.

13. Ibid., p 13.

14. Smith, Goodbye Gutenberg, p 55.

15. James Reston, The Artillery of the Press (New York: Harper and Row, 1966), p 21.

16. Tom Wicker, On Press (New York: The Viking Press, 1978), p 183.

17. Lou Cannon, Reporting: An Inside View (USA: Lou Cannon, 1977), p 45.

18. Wicker, On Press, p 2

19. Jody Powell, Powell and Associates, Washington DC. Interview with the author, 21 December 1983.

20. Tom Wicker, New York Times, New York City. Interview with the author, 15 December 1983.

21. Cannon, Reporting: An Inside View, p 278.

22. Ibid., p 276.

23. Geoffrey Robertson, "Law for the Press" in The British Press: A Manifesto. See pp 207–208 for discussion of both sections of the Official Secrets Act.

24. Henry James, National Association of Pension Funds, London, England. Interview with the author, 7 September 1983.

25. Douglass Cater, The Fourth Branch of Government (Boston: Houghton Mifflin Company, 1959), p 49.

26. Robertson, "Law for the Press," p 204.

27. Anthony Lewis, "Introduction" in None of Your Business, eds. Norman Dorsen and Stephen Gillers (New York: The Viking Press, 1974), p 9.

28. Richard Fryklund, "Covering the Defense Establishment" in The Press in Washington, ed. Ray Eldon Hiebert (New York: Dodd, Mead and Company, 1966), p 167.

29. Anthony Holden, Daily Express, London, England. Interview with the author, 10 September 1983.

30. Ian McDonald, Ministry of Defence, London, England. Interview with the author, 6 September 1983.

31. Cater, The Fourth Branch of Government, p 154.

32. Holden, Interview with the author.

33. James Reston, New York Times, New York City. Telephone conversation with the author, 17 November 1983.

34. Rivers, The Other Government, pp 10–11.

35. Sigal, Reporters and Officials, p 133.

36. The subsequent discussion of Congressional complaints about the press is based largely on Cohen, The Press and Foreign Policy, pp 159–175.

37. Cater, The Fourth Branch of Government, p 31. The relationship between press and President constitutes a primary focus of much writing on the role of the press in America. Some of the better sources for a discussion of this relationship are Cater; Cohen, The Press and Foreign Policy; James Deakin, Straight Stuff: The Reporters, the White House and the Truth (New York: William Morrow, 1984); Reston, The Artillery of the Press; and Wicker, On Press.

38. Cohen, The Press and Foreign Policy, pp 62–63.

39. Reston, The Artillery of the Press, p 89.

40. Hirsch and Gordon, Newspaper Money, p 36.

41. Cannon, Reporting: An Inside View, p 31.

42. Reston, The Artillery of the Press, p 35.

43. David Wise, "Pressures on the Press," in None of Your Business, p 221.

44. Susan Page, Newsday, Long Island NY. Lecture delivered at Harvard University, 30 November 1983.

45. Reston, Artillery of the Press, p 65.

46. Cater, The Fourth Branch of Government, p 65.

2

Press-Government Relations in Britain: The Falklands Crisis

In some senses the Falklands conflict was atypical. It occurred at a distance of 8000 miles, the armed forces controlled access to radio and satellite communications, and hostilities resulted from a special, colonial type of problem which no longer occurs with any frequency either in the United Kingdom or elsewhere. On the other hand,

> The instinctive secrecy of the military and the Civil Service; the prostitution and hysteria of sections of the press; the lies, the misinformation, the manipulation of public opinion by the authorities; the political intimidation of broadcasters; the ready connivance of the media at their own distortion...all these occur as much in normal peace time in Britain as in war.[1]

While the case of the Falklands is not absolutely typical of the British situation in either wartime or peacetime, it does provide an excellent — if admittedly dramatic — context in which to examine the key features of the British press, particularly in its dealings with government.

Even before the Falklands were seized, the Thatcher Government was in an extremely precarious situation, with popularity ratings hovering below 30 percent throughout 1981 and the early months of 1982.[2] When the circumstances surrounding the invasion became known, public outrage mounted to such a pitch that fully one quarter of the respondents in an opinion poll believed that the Prime Minister should resign for failing to prevent the takeover.[3]

Indeed, Britain had had ample warning of Argentina's intentions. On March 19, a group of scrap metal merchants was accompanied to South Georgia (a British dependency 800

21

miles from the Falklands) by a detachment of Argentine Marines who hoisted their national flag and refused to vacate the island. British intelligence chose to ignore this ominous portent of Argentina's military aspirations in the Antarctic. Still more serious, the British Joint Intelligence Committee (JIC) received word on March 26 that an invasion of the Falklands was imminent, but it waited three days to report the information to the Prime Minister and the Cabinet. Nevertheless, by the time the invasion occurred on April 2, Thatcher had been expecting it for four days without taking decisive preventative measures. Even worse, some of her ministers — notably Foreign Secretary Lord Carrington, who subsequently resigned his post — had learned of the anticipated Argentine action a week earlier, with the JIC.

Nor did the Government's actions on April 2 improve its standing in the public eye. Far from moving to challenge the Argentine invaders, during its regular 12:30 pm briefing the Foreign Office refused to confirm news of the invasion, and even denied accurate reports aired by Independent Television News (ITN). By the time the House of Commons met on April 3, in its first Saturday sitting since the Suez crisis of 1956, the Thatcher Government was under heavy attack from Conservative back-benchers and from the Labour Party, which expected to score political points from the Government's failure to prevent the Argentine invasion.

The press, faced with an opportunity to lambaste both the Thatcher Government and Argentina, chose for the most part to focus exclusively on the latter. On April 5 the Times printed an editorial proclaiming, "When British territory is invaded, it is not just an invasion of our land, but of our whole spirit. We are all Falklanders now." (p 9) Newspaper criticisms of government concerned only the secrecy surrounding official responses to the Argentine action. On April 3, the day after the invasion, the Sun — a politically conservative tabloid owned by Australian newspaper magnate Rupert Murdoch — condemned the government for its reticence.

> ...incredibly, it is not yet known what military precautions Britain has taken to safeguard our interests in the Falklands.
>
> The silence in Whitehall yesterday was chilling...
>
> For God's sake, let us have an end to the secrecy that shrouds our policy and intentions.
>
> The Sun's message to Whitehall is a simple and urgent one:
> TELL THE PEOPLE.[6]

Thus the press embarked immediately on the course it was to follow throughout the conflict: enthusiastic support for the government's war effort was accompanied by frustration at official reticence.

JOURNALISTS AND THE TASK FORCE

Initially, in their attempts to keep abreast of developments, newspapers faced an apparently insurmountable obstacle: reliance on a hostile Navy for permission to accompany the task force to the South Atlantic. Navy unfriendliness to the media results from three factors. First, unlike the Army, which deals constantly with the press in Northern Ireland, the Navy has no familiarity and consequently no rapport with journalists. Second, shipboard existence fosters a claustrophobic attitude which looks with extreme suspicion on attempts to publicize Navy activities. Finally, the Navy — more than other branches of the armed forces — suffers from defense cuts prompted by bad press.[4]

Accreditation

At first, therefore, the Navy refused to accredit any journalists to sail with the task force. Sensitive to the need for good publicity as well as to military considerations, however, the Ministry of Defence (MoD) refused to let the flotilla travel under a complete news blackout. Unfortunately, the MoD permitted the National Publishers' Association (NPA) to choose the five lucky journalists. Established in 1906 to handle industrial relations, printing, and distribution among the national press, the NPA has had little impact on the media. Former Defence Secretary John Nott regards it as an incompetent body.[5] Perhaps the MoD was unaware of the NPA's poor reputation, or perhaps Defence officials were concerned only to guarantee the presence of reporters with the task force and cared little for the manner of their selection. In any case, the NPA's procedure for selecting the reporters to accompany the task force was questionable: "The head of the NPA held a sort of garden party and plucked the names out of a hat," recalls Ian McDonald, official MoD spokesman during the Falklands crisis.[6]

When the names of the lottery winners were revealed, it became clear that chance had done poorly by the media: neither the quality titles nor the most popular tabloids had been chosen. Publishers, editors, and individual reporters from newspapers that were not selected began complaining vociferously to contacts in Whitehall and the MoD. Some of these contacts took up the journalists' cause because they recognized the advantages for Government of publicizing a military expedition that by all odds would be extremely successful. Others agreed to work toward establishing more reporters on the task force because they realized that relations between government and the press would be damaged irremediably if reporters from important newspapers were excluded from an event of great national significance. When Bernard Ingham, press secretary for No. 10 Downing Street, went to bat for the press, the Navy could hold out no longer. Ultimately, 29 journalists accompanied the task force to the South Atlantic.

However, the foreign press obtained no accreditation. Lacking domestic political influence, representatives of foreign newspapers could not lobby Whitehall and the MoD. Not only did foreign journals lack an effective voice for communicating their needs; more importantly, they were regarded with suspicion by the British Government. According to John Witherow, the Times correspondent with the task force, the MoD expected of British reporters a degree of sympathy to the war effort that would not be shared by the foreign press. "They wanted us there merely as propagandists. They looked upon me as some kind of Fifth Columnist"[7] when he broached the subject of objectivity in reporting. Indeed, foreign journalists were not permitted entry to official MoD briefings until three weeks after the Argentine invasion, and even then they were excluded from the informal daily briefings provided for British defense correspondents.

Former No. 10 Downing Street press secretary Henry James admits that the exclusion of foreign reporters created the semblance of bias. "People tend to make assumptions that the national media are part of the structure of the country,"[8] avows Mr. James, and consequently accuse the government of conducting a propaganda campaign on its own behalf. It is not implausible, claims Mr. James, that the presence of foreign journalists could have provided skeptical observers — the governments of France and Spain, for example — with a "compass bearing" by which to measure the verity of British claims.

Some government officials blame the British press itself for the exclusion of foreign reporters from the task force. Eager for their own journalists to accompany the fleet, newspapers refused to choose a pool of correspondents to file stories for general use, and consequently took all the places available to the press, leaving none for foreign reporters. In the general chaos surrounding the struggle for accreditation, officials claim that they failed to understand the gravity of this omission.[9]

The speed with which the task force was dispatched precluded not only careful consideration of the usefulness of foreign correspondents but also intelligent selection of journalists for accreditation. The House of Commons Defence Committee found that

> One by-product of the speed with which the press party was selected was that the press and broadcasting organizations had to select their representatives from whoever was immediately available rather than being able to choose their most experienced war reporters.[10]

As a result, few of the journalists dispatched to the Falklands had prior experience of war reporting. Most of them were physically unfit, and their assumption that the task force would engage in a bit of gunboat diplomacy and then return to England prevented them from acquiring adequate provisions for an arduous military campaign in the Antarctic.

Still worse, because military service is no longer compulsory in Britain, few of the journalists had served in the armed forces, and consequently they were completely unfamiliar with Navy procedures and attitudes. Embarked reporters refused to acknowledge the fact that "the primary purpose of a task force," in the words of Mr. James, is to supply political — and, if necessary, military — pressure. One Government spokesman criticizes journalists with the task force for failing to adapt psychologically to a war situation and for insisting that their own requirements receive top priority attention. Such presumptuousness, according to this source, alienated military personnel who otherwise might have been perfectly friendly.[11]

Competition Among Journalists

Certainly Navy fears were not assuaged when the fierce competition which had begun in London among newspapers anxious to secure positions with the task force escalated among journalists very shortly after the fleet left Portsmouth. Hungry for exciting information that simply was not generated during two weeks at sea, the reporters "churned out editorials, commentaries, and reports, in that order of priority." The attempt to formulate different dispatches where no scope for difference existed spawned ill will and extremist styles among reporters. As Mr. James comments, "The most appalling jingoistic headlines were really just contrived to fill the gaps between 'local boy' stories." John Witherow recalls that "We wrote daily, and there was often nothing to write about." The progress of peace talks further threatened the ability of embarked journalists to find titillating information for publication. As one observer wryly commented,

> Nothing is so fatal to reader interest in a good war as the threat of peace, and this time it came at an awkward juncture. With the British fleet still weeks from its objective, and the Falklands kelpers themselves cut off from inspection, communication lines to reader interest were already dangerously extended.[13]

Thus the inherent bias of the media toward competitive sensationalism was strengthened by the circumstances of reporters with the task force.

Nor did the situation improve once the fleet reached its destination, although journalists did display willingness to withhold information for security reasons after the fighting began. ITN correspondent John Underwood explains that the reporters "were under immense pressure, and finding that they were physically unfit and mentally unprepared led them to daggers at each others' throats."[14] Indeed, Max Hastings — a correspondent with the Standard whose familiarity with war reporting and rapport with Navy personnel resulted in his filing a great deal more and better copy than the other reporters — was physically attacked by an angry fellow journalist after the task force docked in Port Stanley. Such desperate competition was grounded in several serious problems.

Technical Difficulties

First, correspondents attempting to dispatch copy to their London editors were hampered by the limitations of satellite communications aboard a flotilla in the South Atlantic. As Henry James explains, "When you have to assemble a task force in 48 hours, getting a television camera on on board is not your highest priority." So long as the task force had not reached the Falklands, press dispatches were transmitted over the ships' military communications systems, which already were overburdened by heavy operational traffic. Once the troops invaded the islands, reporters who accompanied them could transmit dispatches to the ships with communications equipment only by soliciting the favor of Army helicopter pilots who flew regularly between the task force and the ground troops. Many correspondents chose to remain on shipboard, then, where the chances of transmitting their stories were better. On the other hand, at least one reporter felt that staying close to communications equipment rather than accompanying the invading forces was akin to "being locked in the loo at a Royal garden party while outside the Queen Mother was performing cartwheels."[15]

Without a doubt, technical difficulties did affect relations between reporters and the military with the task force. Normally, correspondents are based on land; they are provided with extensive communications facilities, and even in case of breakdown they can devise some means of removing their copy from the war zone. They can slip across the border to a neighboring country or use the telex in a nearby hotel or enlist the aid of a friendly citizen. In the Antarctic, none of these possibilities existed: journalists were completely at the mercy of the Navy.

Military Non-Cooperation

The relevant issue, then, is military treatment of dependent reporters, particularly as disagreement rages about the extent to which technical shortcomings were the true cause of correspondents' inability to file copy. For example, although transmission of television film was deemed completely impossible, television coverage had occurred in similar circumstances during other wars.[16] John Witherow claims that Navy protestations about the infeasibility of providing better satellite systems were "bollocks," and even a high-ranking Government spokesman concedes that communications difficulties were not the primary problem.[17]

The primary problem, on the contrary, was the grudging attitude of the military when confronted with the spectre of journalistic busybodies. As Witherow notes in the book which he co-authored with Patrick Bishop of the Observer,

The Navy would have preferred a private encounter with Argentina with the occasional release in London to say South Georgia or the Falklands had been retaken....We had been warned, though. At the outset we were told there was a conflict of interests. Our job was to disseminate news, the ministry's [MoD's] was to suppress it. It was an axiom which proved all too accurate.[18]

Communications difficulties merely compounded fundamental hostility to journalists travelling with the fleet. From the outset the Navy had attempted to bar reporters, so it came as no surprise that — in the words of the Defence Committee — "not all the officers appreciated some of the aspects of the journalists' position."[19] Indeed, Navy commanders were so unfriendly to the press that official briefings occurred irregularly while the usual informal flow of information was reduced to a mere trickle.[20]

Such tight control was possible because mistrust of the media extended to the rank-and-file.

Men worried deeply about their families at home, and how bad news might be affecting them. They cursed the broadcasters and newspaper photographers when they believed that news and pictures were being released in Britain which would cause fear or pain.[21]

As a result, low-ranking troops were no more cooperative toward journalists than were their superiors. In short, the unwillingness of Navy personnel at all levels to assist journalists figured far more prominently than did technical difficulties in the limitations on information dispatched from the task force.

Censorship

Particularly irksome to reporters was the assignment of censorship tasks to minders, low-ranking MoD public relations officers who were accustomed only to answering telephone inquiries and arranging journalists' visits to military sites.[22] Insufficiently well-informed about military affairs to make their own decisions, the minders generally sought guidance from Navy senior officials. Reliance on military advice slowed the dispatch process and irritated Navy personnel, who attached little importance to the needs of reporters.[23] Worse still, occasionally the minders chose to exercise initiative; in such cases, "they believed that 'better safe than sorry' was the right attitude for them to hold, and as a result sometimes vetted copy over-cautiously."[24]   On May 14, Daily Mirror columnist Alistair MacQueen wrote,

> On the odd occasion when we have been able to send news stories, they have either been censored into gibberish or delayed so long in transmission they have arrived in London much too late for deadlines. (p 3)

In addition to needlessly restricting the flow of news off the task force, John Witherow complains, minders refused to share with reporters their MoD directives concerning censorship.   Thus the minders, who — by establishing and insisting upon the observance of clear behavioral guidelines for both sides — could have served to ease interactions between journalists and Navy personnel, instead comprised an additional source of friction.

The minders were no more popular for the fact that they represented only the way-station en route to MoD censorship in London.   According to the Defence Committee, the justification for dual censorship involved

> the fact that there were local security concerns which had to be taken into account in addition to those affecting the military operations in their totality, and that censors in London could not necessarily have been aware of all these local factors.[25]

Not everyone in government was satisfied with the arrangement, however.   Some MoD officials protested vehemently the decision to re-censor in London material that had been approved on site.   With events in the South Atlantic transpiring at a rapid pace, they maintained, London-based personnel lacked the current information that would permit them to function effectively as censors; their activities served merely to foster bad relations with the press.[26]

Journalists were particularly perturbed by the inconsistency and illogic of the censorship operation.   Often it appeared that task force minders and London censors were working at cross purposes, or that MoD orders to minders contravened Navy interests.[27]   Still worse, sensitive information that was carefully deleted from task force dispatches appeared on newspaper front pages because it had been leaked by MoD officials in London.   A reporter with ITN complains that "There seemed to be no coordination between what we were being told in London and what the task force reporters were allowed to say."[28]   The _Times_ of June 9 printed the statement by Max Hastings, with the fleet, that

> all the serious lapses of security have taken place in London, where at times it seems that the MoD has taken leave of its senses in announcing forthcoming operations. (p 10)

Task force journalists were infuriated when stories which had been obtained and filed at great personal risk were censored by over-zealous minders and then released anyway as the result of MoD indiscretion in London.

In several instances, inconsistent censorship damaged more than journalists' tempers. On May 28, the BBC World Service reported that the 2 Para regiment was two miles from Goose Green; probably as a result, the Argentine garrison at Goose Green was reinforced before the British forces invaded. Aboard the task force, where troops and officers alike believed that the BBC correspondents with the fleet had leaked the information, resentment of the BBC was overwhelming.[29]

GOVERNMENT AND THE JOURNALISTS IN LONDON

Soon, however, it became clear that the leak had originated with indiscreet MoD officials in London, where relations between government and the press were no friendlier than on the task force. John Underwood explains that throughout the war, the Government was obliged to make statements to its supporters about the progress of the British forces — often, as in this case, prematurely — in order to retain political backing. Government statements generally were not made available to the media, but the House of Commons and the MoD were filled with people who knew quite a lot, and under pressure from journalists, these officials revealed material of often critical sensitivity. Mr. Underwood recalls that "in the excitement of the moment... both places were leaking like hell...it was almost like a bazaar of information."

Government officials offer alternative interpretations of the breach of security surrounding the Goose Green invasion. According to one government spokesman, the leak resulted not from indiscretion but from the fact that Army representatives in the MoD were "fed up" with taking a back seat to the Navy in newspaper coverage. By leaking information about an imminent Army maneuver, they hoped to win public recognition of the role of ground forces in the fighting.[30] Sir John Nott maintains that news of the invasion appeared prematurely not because — for whatever reason — the BBC received a tip-off from government officials but because of clever speculation by the network's military experts. John Witherow counters that "Goose Green was a completely illogical move militarily" so it is highly implausible that the BBC made a lucky guess about the plans of troops in the area.

The Ministry of Defence

It is likely, particularly given the MoD's susceptibility to leaks, that premature news of the Goose Green attack resulted from indiscretion in some branch of government. Since the beginning of the crisis, MoD arrangements for briefing London journalists had been conducive to indiscretion. At the outset, the public relations department at the MoD banned all contacts between Ministry staffers and the media except for a single daily briefing by official MoD spokesman Ian McDonald, whose appearance on television screens throughout Britain catapulted him to overnight stardom. Peeved at being effectively muzzled, and harassed by journalists frantic for news, MoD officials failed to honor the embargo on unofficial information.[31]

The situation was not improved by journalists' dislike of Mr. McDonald, who was serving temporarily as Chief of Public Relations until the new chief could assume his duties. For one thing, Mr. McDonald was an administrative civil servant rather than a public relations expert, so his familiarity with the media was minimal. As Mr. James asserts, "There should have been a professional director of information in the MoD from Day One." (In fact, not until mid-May — halfway through the crisis — did the new chief take over.) For another thing, Mr. McDonald's unschooled efforts to appear impartial led journalists attending his briefings to conclude that "he seemed more like a maiden aunt than a government representative."[32] Indeed, a Times reporter complained on May 6 that "The mechanical way in which he speaks is mystifying and even a little sinister." (p 2) On May 31, the Daily Mirror demanded, "Is there some sinister purpose behind the continuing TV appearances of Ian (Batteries Not Included) McDonald?" (p 10)

Even after the MoD opened a 24-hour Emergency Press Centre on May 2, in an effort to deal with overwhelming demand for news and also to shift attention away from McDonald, relations between journalists and the information officials did not progress satisfactorily. In his report to the Defence Committee, one ITN executive described Centre staffers as

> information officers who could not answer our questions because they were not of high enough rank....The briefing room manager (a duty press officer) would announce that a statement was on its way, but his prognostication of when was never correct.[33]

Although the officers in the Centre were empowered to refer journalists with questions to more knowledgeable sources, the MoD's emergency information hierarchy was so complicated that only highly experienced defense correspondents with prior knowledge of the Ministry knew which officials would have the information they wanted.[34]

There seems to have been little justification for these complications beyond the fact that MoD officials jealous of their prerogatives were reluctant to relinquish responsibility to a central information bureau, particularly one headed by a newcomer to the field of public relations. When Mr. McDonald became Chief of Public Relations, he assumed jurisdiction over an office staffed by professional public relations officers who resented being subordinated to a novice. Consequently,

> Tensions built up strongly between the civil servants who were controlling the information, the military PR men who thought they should be controlling it, and the poor "Desk officers" in the Press Office, who knew nothing, said nothing, and received much of the flack (sic) from the press corps for the Ministry's reticence.[35]

In the words of Henry James, "the journalists left behind [in London] had a lot to complain about."

And complain they did. However, neither the correspondents who sailed with the task force nor their colleagues in London found fault with the principle of censorship, and few grumbled about the injustice of dual censorship. Journalist Anthony Holden comments, "I think in any democratic society the government has a right to conceal information which would damage the national interest."[36] John Witherow affirms that "censorship is essential in time

of war...But it's got to be done in an intelligent way."
Thus journalists were perturbed only by the inefficiency and
confusion with which censorship was exercised.

When officials lodged specific requests, journalists
readily agreed to withhold news. Anthony Barnett explains,

> The press criticised censorship not because it took
> place but because it made the media look stupid.
> In effect the editors were asking that the MoD
> take them into its confidence and allow them to
> help in the censorship process. They were of-
> fended at being treated as an enemy.[37]

Indeed, by agreeing not to identify news stories as Censored,
editors complied tacitly with the government, which wanted
no publicity about censorship to mar its avowed commitment
to democratic principles. As a journalist remarks in a 1983
London play, Falkland Sound/Voces de Malvinas, "If I had
been filing from Poland at that time, all my stories would
have been marked 'Censored.' But how many pieces filed
from the South Atlantic were marked like that? Not one."[38]

Because journalists liked to regard themselves as
patriots and had no desire to damage the war effort by publishing information which might damage national security,
they objected strenuously to MoD attempts to mislead them.
Instances in which the Ministry deliberately misinformed
reporters are too numerous to list fully, and in any case the
Defence Committee report states that "the Ministry of
Defence have freely admitted, and without apology, that they
did not always tell the whole truth."[39] One of the more
blatant cases of misinformation concerns the Port Stanley
airfield, which was subjected to a British bombing attack
early in the war. In his Defence Committee evidence, one
ITN executive reported,

> Constantly we were told the runway had been
> bombed and the impression was left that it was
> out of action. The need for further bombing raids
> altered that impression though never at any time
> was any information passed out that came
> anywhere near the truth.[40]

In fact, the bombers had missed the airfield altogether.

If journalists were angered by the MoD's failure to
report accurately on the Port Stanley runway — a breach
explained in terms of tactical military considerations — they
were infuriated by information management that smacked of

political propagandizing. The Defence Committee report
queries rhetorically,

> Was it just by chance that the celebrated picture
> of San Carlos villagers offering a Marine a cup of
> tea achieved such instant currency, while others
> such as the one of HMS Antelope exploding suf-
> fered considerable delays?[41]

The Glasgow Media Group conclude that "the Ministry of
Defence did want to censor and not just for the purposes of
operational secrecy."[42]

Government officials contest such allegations
vehemently. Henry James avows that "there was no
censorship, and no attempt at censorship," for political
purposes. Almost always, officials maintain, failure to disclose information promptly resulted either from security considerations or from the desire to avoid releasing news until
the families of the wounded had been personally notified.
Ian McDonald recounts some of the difficulties involved in
informing the next of kin:

> Of course when a ship goes down all its papers go
> down too, and you don't know which men are off
> at the dentist or were flown home or what. And
> then you have a situation like the Welsh Guards,
> which was made up entirely of men called Jones,
> and you have to get all the Joneses sorted out.

Toward the end of the war, under increasing media pressure,
the MoD adopted the attitude that "the next of kin might
be on holiday in Bavaria" and abandoned efforts to notify
family members before releasing bad news to the press.

In fact, it is questionable whether censorship was exercised only for reasons of military security or kindness to
family members, because in many cases the emotions of
families were utterly disregarded. When HMS Galahad was
hit, the Sun noted on June 11 that Nott's "delay in giving
the most realistic total of casualties, even two days after
the attack, meant more hours of agony for the wives,
mothers and sweethearts of the 9,000 Falklands servicemen."
(p 1) As John Witherow recalls, the MoD tried to lull Argentina into a false sense of safety by announcing falsely
high casualties for the Galahad. "All the time they'd been
bleating on about the next of kin, and then this...They would
argue that this was part of supporting the military effort."

Ironically, heavy censorship by the MoD may well have

done more to hinder the war effort than to advance it. Unable to acquire information from official sources, British journalists were driven for news to two unreliable agents. First, the press called in retired defense experts to comment on the war. Most of these experts were unaccustomed to the practiced probes of trained interviewers, and as a result they let slip information which truly could have jeopardized the safety of the task force. For example, a retired Air Force officer gave instructions detailing the proper procedure to shoot down a British Sea Harrier with a Mirage, one of the planes used by Argentina.[43]

Less dangerous, but more offensive to the government, was the media's increasing use of Argentine war reports as a source of factual information.[44] As early as April 6, the Sun reproduced Argentine photographs of British Marines surrendering in Port Stanley (pp 4-5). As hostilities continued, dismay mounted in Britain about the amount of air time and page space devoted to Argentine reports. On May 11, the Sun stated,

> PROTESTS that Defence bosses are slow to give Britain all the facts about the fighting were discussed yesterday by Premier Margaret Thatcher's war cabinet.
> Sometimes Argentina has been first to report war developments while Whitehall has held back its version for hours. (p 2)

As the Daily Mirror pointed out on June 11, "If we are slow to tell the truth, then people will be quick to think there is something in Argentina's lies." (p 2)

No. 10 Downing Street

Recognizing the adverse effects of ill-conceived, inconsistent, heavy censorship, Bernard Ingham and other officials at No. 10 Downing Street disapproved strongly of the MoD's attempts to mislead and muzzle the press.

> One of the features of the so-called "information war" was that everyone fought everyone else: Whitehall fought the Navy, the Government fought Whitehall, all three fought the media, and the media...fought among themselves.[45]

Only three times did dissatisfaction at No. 10 cause the MoD to change its policies, however. The first instance took place at the outset of the crisis, when No. 10 press secretary Bernard Ingham forced the accreditation of 23 journalists more than had been anticipated originally. The second instance occurred in April, when the task force had been at sea for more than a week but no photographs had appeared in the press. Soon thereafter, a few blurred prints of British troops on shipboard made their way into the newspapers.[46] The third time officials at No. 10 expressed displeasure, MoD background briefings — which had been halted at the start of the crisis — were resumed.[47]

Simply because the Prime Minister's office was dissatisfied with the MoD's handling of the media, it should not be inferred that No. 10 championed the ideals of a free press during the crisis. On the contrary, the Government was concerned to see the British case presented as convincingly as possible; objections to MoD behavior stemmed only from the observation that the Ministry's blunders contributed little to the desired image of Britain as a beleaguered but stalwart innocent.

Indeed, in May the BBC was viciously attacked in the House of Commons for failing to cooperate in selling Britain's case to the public at home and abroad. Noting that BBC news programs did not refer to British troops as "our forces," and that one broadcast had listed Argentine claims to the Falklands, Thatcher commented darkly in the House of Commons that "the case for our British forces is not being put over fully and effectively."[48] MPs were less restrained in their criticism. On May 12, the chairman and the Director General-designate of the BBC were summoned to the House of Commons and lambasted for over an hour in a manner which later prompted observers to describe the scene as "blood and entrails all over the place," "they were roasted alive," "the ugliest meeting I have ever attended in my years as an MP."[49] Recalling the vitriol, Ian McDonald comments, "If you had seen those broadcasts you really wouldn't have understood what everyone was making such a fuss about. They were very bland: nothing, really." Actually, a great deal was at stake.

During wartime a conflict of interests frequently arises between the government and the BBC, because the state does not always appreciate the BBC's firm commitment to the principle of objective reporting.[50] Sir John Nott states vehemently that the BBC's exaggerated view of its own importance prompted the network to stage debates concerning an issue which never should have been contested: namely, the merit of British claims to the Falklands. According to Sir John, the young producers and directors of the BBC are unfamiliar with wartime situations and fail to respond with appropriate patriotism when challenged by the novel experience. Clearly, the implication is that no national news forum has any business debating — not to mention decisively contesting, which the BBC never presumed to do — the advisability of a war which is being conducted by the government. When it does, in the words of John Underwood, "balance and equity and fairness go straight out the window."

In defending itself, the BBC argued principally that the impossibility of obtaining information and newsfilm from the MoD had forced broadcasters to air programs based on any available news sources. The _Times_ of May 7 reported "pained reactions from many editors that the MoD, by delay and reticence over important news developments, was damaging the credibility of both the Government and the media," (p 5) while the _Daily Mirror_ recalled on May 11 that "the BBC had repeatedly pointed out to the MoD the urgency of making arrangements for sending pictures from the task force back to Britain." (p 1)

As the rhetoric mounted, the Prince of Wales, 81 percent of the voting public, and every national newspaper save the _Sun_ came out in favor of the BBC's right to report objectively.[51] The _Guardian_ commented on May 12 that "Our television and radio channels...have been doing the best they can in appallingly (sometimes wilfully) difficult circumstances." (p 2) The _Daily Mirror_ editorialized on the same day that "The Government is trying to bludgeon the BBC into becoming a mouthpiece for its Falklands policy. The BBC should fight it." (p 2) Several weeks later, on May 31, _Mirror_ columnist Keith Waterhouse denounced the BBC's detractors as an "etymological junta" exercising "squatting rights" over the word patriotism. (p 10) Faced with such overwhelming support for the embattled BBC, the government backed down, not without one last statement by Foreign Minister Francis Pym that the lack of available newsfilm did not excuse BBC coverage of the war.[52]

The BBC conflict nicely illustrates the government's tendency during the Falklands conflict to reinforce the general hyper-patriotic slant of the media. For the most part, as will be discussed below, this bias was created in the hopes of attracting readers in a highly competitive market. Ironically, it is debatable whether public enthusiasm matched the nationlist fervor displayed by the press.

JINGOISM IN THE PRESS

In 1982 Britain supported eight national daily and eight national Sunday newspapers. Within each of the two categories, titles struggled fiercely to increase their readership. Throughout 1981, the national tabloids introduced lotteries, bingo contests and other gimmicks designed to boost circulation.[53] When Argentina invaded the Falklands, newspapers seized on the event as a serendipitous drama that would certainly capture reader attention and sell copy. Competition for scoops and exclusives, intense under normal conditions, became frantic when all available news was channeled through a government agency that refused to give unofficial briefings and parcelled out information with an impartially stingy hand.

Faced with the impossibility of differing factually from its competitors, each newspaper strove to differentiate itself by printing uniquely vehement, eye–catching headlines and articles. Of Britain's eight national dailies, five are tabloids and three are quality newspapers. In both categories, all but one of the titles have conservative editorial policies, and therefore faced no dilemma by backing the Tory war effort. Consequently, as one observer noted at the time,

> the bulk of the British media has been reporting the Falklands crisis on a stereotype born of Hollywood out of the Second World War. As if on some archaic autopilot, the tabloid press has cartwheeled across the sky.[54]

On April 12, long before peace negotiations finally broke down, the Sun editorialized, "We do not want war, but if there is no other way — GIVE THEM HELL, MAGGIE!" (P 6) On the first of May, under the headline "Stick This Up Your Junta!", the Sun announced a fund–raiser wherein contributors' names were written on missiles fired at Argentine planes. (p 2) When British guns sank the Argentine cruiser Belgrano, the Sun headline of May 4 exulted "Gotcha!", and the accompanying story began, "The Navy had the Argies on their knees last night." (p 1) On May 11, the Sun identified itself on page one as the "PAPER THAT SUPPORTS OUR BOYS," and continued to carry the logo until the end of the war.

With the exception of the Guardian, quality titles commended the war effort with more restraint but with no less nationalist fervor then the tabloids displayed. The Telegraph and the Times endorsed the expedition wholeheartedly; indeed, the Times and the Sun, both titles owned by Rupert Murdoch, "together conducted a daily pincer movement on opinion."[55] Despite assurances that the Times would remain editorially independent, Murdoch brought the paper into line with his other publications. Nevertheless, its continued status as a quality title prevented it from achieving the popularity enjoyed by the Sun.[56]

At the same time, the Times also failed to realize its promise of rational, objective reporting, and instead delivered watered-down jingoism. As early as April 21, an editorial encouraging peace negotiations contained the significant proviso that compromise would be acceptable "only in accordance with first principles." (p 13) When the Belgrano was sunk, the Times applauded, querying on May 5, "What, after all, is the British task force doing there?" (p 11) On May 22, when hostilities were in full swing, an editorial advised the English people that "we must untie with our teeth a knot that would not yield to the tongue." (p 11)

Newspapers which did not endorse the war effort failed to achieve the level of rhetoric displayed by pro-war publications. The Guardian, which is Britain's sole left-wing quality daily, enjoyed the distinction of being the only quality title opposed to military intervention. However, even the Guardian did little more than quietly counsel the government to exercise restraint by exhausting all available channels of compromise before using force.

On the other hand, by registering any disapproval of the war effort, the Guardian distinguished itself from the mass of the Left. In the early stages of the crisis, the Right commandeered key phrases like "nationalism" and "sovereignty," thereby limiting the lexicon of terms available to the Labour Party, which strove to reconcile a pacifist liberal outlook with the desire to ride the wave of perceived public patriotism. Recognizing the electoral inadvisability of opposition to the government when the task force sailed, Labour came out in favor of the war effort.

Labour's support for the use of force in the Falklands created an awkward situation for the tabloid Daily Mirror, with which the Labour Party is closely aligned both ideologically and institutionally. On the one hand, the Mirror did not want to betray its commitment to liberal opposition and pacifism by supporting the Government; on the other hand, the newspaper was reluctant to disagree with its parent Party, much less to risk losing readers by coming out against the war. Thus the Mirror toed a narrow line somewhere between strong and mild objection to the military effort, moving further away from wholehearted disapproval as the task force registered success and victory seemed certain.

On April 8, the <u>Mirror</u> scoffed, "Mrs. Thatcher's answer to Not the Nine O'Clock News, Nott the Defence Secretary, has made a feeble attempt to resign. (Can't he do <u>anything</u> right?)" (p 12) However, on April 20 the newspaper adopted the attitude that the use of force to regain the Falklands would be justified if negotiations failed (p 3), and thereafter <u>Mirror</u> editorials criticized Argentina more often than they reproved the Thatcher Government.

The <u>Mirror</u>'s lukewarm opposition to the war did not prevent it from being the subject of vicious attack by the <u>Sun</u>. On April 2, the <u>Sun</u> offered to "<u>arrange a free sub-</u> <u>scription to the sinking Daily Mirror</u>" (p 6) for everyone who counselled against military involvement in the Falklands. On April 6, a <u>Sun</u> editorial sneered that

> The ailing Daily Mirror, which tried to pretend that there was no threat to the Falklands until the invaders had actually landed, now whines that we should give in to force and obligingly settle the is-landers elsewhere. (p 6)

At the height of the brouhaha over the BBC, the <u>Sun</u> printed a diatribe against media failing to register full sup-port for the war effort.

Dare Call It Treason

> There are traitors in our midst.
> Margaret Thatcher talked about them in the House of Commons yesterday.
> She referred to those newspapers and com-mentators on radio and TV who are not properly conveying Britain's case over the Falklands, and who are treating this country as if she and the Argentines had an equal claim to justice, con-sideration and loyalty.
> The Prime Minister did not speak of treason. <u>The Sun does not hesitate to use the word</u>....
> We are caught up in a shooting war not a game of croquet. There are no neutral referees above the sound of the guns. A British citizen is either on his country's side — or he is its enemy....
> The Daily Mirror...has pretensions as a mass sale newspaper.
> What is it but treason for this timorous, whining publication to plead day after day for

appeasing the Argentine dictators because they do
not believe the British people have the stomach
for a fight, and are instead prepared to trade
peace for honour? (p 6)

Thus the <u>Sun</u> threw down the gauntlet in no uncertain terms.
For its part, the <u>Daily Mirror</u> proved equal to the
challenge.

The Harlot of Fleet Street

The Sun, a coarse and demented newspaper,
yesterday accused The Daily Mirror, the Guardian
and...the BBC of being traitors to Britain.
What The Sun means by treachery is a
refusal to twist, distort and mangle the truth
about the fighting in the South Atlantic.
No one could accuse The Sun of failing to
do that. (p 2)

The invective that flew between the two newspapers
prompted one observer to comment that "Fleet Street
tabloids dispense editorial abuse as casually as their
American counterparts condemn litter in the parks."[57]
Another commentator remarked, ironically, that

for years to come the first five weeks of conflict
between Britain and Argentina [will] furnish a
textbook example for journalistic training schools
and staff colleges, not to mention Nieman seminars
and Aspen folkmoots, of how war should be fought
in the press.[58]

Actually, the two tabloids were engaged in a war: the war
for higher circulation.
During the Falklands crisis the Government, the Opposition, and most newspapers shared the assumption that the
public backed the war effort unilaterally and enthusiastically,
and explained their own actions accordingly. Labour
politicians justified their support for the war by invoking the
"nationalist and backward looking, imperial longings of the
working class."[59] Journalist Anthony Holden expressed a
common sentiment among reporters with the comment that
"the media responded to the public mood — with some
surprise, of course, that the public mood was so intense."

With hindsight, however, it is possible to see that public approbation for the war effort may not have been so pronounced as was generally supposed. Certainly editorial policy had little effect on newspaper circulation. All their posturing and vitriol notwithstanding, the national dailies registered similar increases in readership throughout the Falklands crisis. In fact, in June the Guardian — whose anti-war stance prompted predictions of heavy losses — gained nearly 50,000 readers over its June 1981 total. On the other side of the political spectrum, the Times also showed a growth in readership figures.[60]

At the same time, opinion polls conducted for the Economist indicated strong but not unanimous support for the war effort. On April 17, 49 percent of respondents answered negatively when queried, "Do you think that retaining sovereignty over the Falklands is important enough to justify the loss of British servicemen's lives?" (Forty-four percent responded affirmatively to this question.) A full 39 percent of respondents favored "joint Argentine/British administration over the Falklands with US overseers and the islanders involved."[61] As late as May 25, the Thatcher Government was described by fully 25 percent of poll respondents as being "too willing to use military force" in the crisis. (Sixty-four percent of respondents characterized the Government's attitude toward military force as "about right.")[62] At the close of the war, on June 26, although 76 percent of poll respondents answered affirmatively to the question "Given the cost in lives and money, do you think Britain should have sent the task force or not?", nearly a quarter of respondents believed that the task force never should have been sent.[63]

These figures, combined with evidence of the increased circulations of the Guardian and the Daily Mirror, suggest that the public was not wholeheartedly in favor of the military effort. Undoubtedly the public was interested in the war, but the extent to which interest involved fervent feelings of patriotism is debatable. People who habitually read the Daily Mirror were content to continue doing so, because the Mirror contained as much war news as any other tabloid. The same holds true for Guardian readers. Thus it is arguable that "the headlines were larger than their readers' emotions"[64]: that — far from following public enthusiasm — what Henry James calls the media's "reaction of shock, horror, appallment that this could be done to us, to Britons and to two million sheep" served to create public interest in the war effort.

CONCLUSION

Media competition, then, exerts a considerable effect on the news in Britain. The national press, troubled by the need to boost circulation in a saturated market, welcomed the Argentine invasion of the Falklands as a unique opportunity to captivate reader interest. Editorial dismay when peace negotiations advanced, and encouragement for military bravado, were too pronounced to ignore.

> The tabloid press...was continuing to run pages of near-hysterical war-mongering...Fleet Street's yearning for an old-fashioned sea battle was equalled only by its suspicion that the Foreign Office might be conspiring to cheat it of one.[65]

More than anything, the newspaper industry did not want the government to negotiate an end to the conflict that was proving so lucrative.

The newspaper industry, however, should have known it had nothing to fear. The Thatcher Government was no less delighted than the press by the unexpected advent of an opportunity to boost its popularity among the public. The Falklands conflict transformed one of the least popular prime ministers since World War Two into the most popular.[66] Had the press and the government realized the extent of their mutual interest, they could have collaborated directly to extract the maximum possible benefit from islands "about which nothing was known, invaded with legal justifications no one could understand, and defended with an ardor no one could fathom."[67]

The media did make some overtures to the government. From the outset of the crisis, newspapers refrained from criticizing Thatcher for her failure to act on advance notice of the invasion, and instead confined themselves to censuring Argentina. On the task force, British journalists lived closely with the British military and were personally endangered by an enemy of Britain. As a result, embarked journalists were more willing than might be expected to withhold news that could endanger the task force. Ian McDonald recounts the story of one reporter with the fleet who decided not to report a failed British attack because "the captain with his stomach shot away, this chap had been having drinks with him just the night before." Even in London, where the incentive to do so was minimal, journalists were prepared to exercise self-restraint.

Because negative attitudes toward the press prevail among officials in Britain, however, the government failed to take the hint. To the bitter end, when news of Argentina's defeat was withheld from journalists for nearly 12 hours (until it could be announced in the House of Commons),[68] the government proved itself hostile to and distrustful of the media. Throughout the conflict, the press was regarded as an inconvenience; consequently, its demands for accreditation, for improved communications facilities, and for consistent censorship were granted grudgingly, if at all. Journalists travelling with the task force were required to adapt uncomplainingly to very difficult conditions, and were excoriated when they did not. Reporters covering events at the MoD were expected to refrain from attempting to augment their meagre news diet, which consisted only of a single daily briefing. The BBC was lambasted simply for enumerating Argentine claims to the Falklands.

Such attitudes reflect the fact that government in Britain is accustomed to its position of superiority in dealings with the press. Legal restrictions on the media are effective and rarely challenged by journalists. The state is not habituated to treating the media as an equal. In general, the media does not request such a high degree of respect, but the Falklands crisis was a unique case. Newspapers wanted desperately to support the government and its war effort, but from the outset they were excluded from the excitement. Reduced to a single official briefing daily, they resorted to sensationalistic coverage. In Britain, a state accustomed to secrecy has not come to terms with an intensely competitive national press seeking through lurid reportage to attract readers and boost circulation.

1. Robert Harris, Gotcha! The Media, the Government and the Falklands Crisis (Boston: Faber and Faber, Inc., 1983), p 151.

2. "We Like It So Far," Economist (Vol 283, No 7234, 24 April 1982), p 27.

3. "British Politics: Off On A Wrong Foot," Economist (Vol 283, No 7232, 10 April 1982), p 21.

4. John Witherow, Times, London, England. Interview with the author, 8 September 1983.

5. John Nott, Lazard Brothers, London, England. Interview with the author, 6 September 1983. All subsequent remarks by Sir John are taken from this interview.

6. Ian McDonald, Ministry of Defence, London, England. Interview with Deborah Holmes, 6 September 1983. All subsequent remarks by Mr. McDonald are taken from this interview. See also Harris, Gotcha!, p 19; and Defence Committee, "The Handling of Press," p xxxvi.

7. John Witherow, Interview with the author. All subsequent remarks by Mr. Witherow, unless noted as being from his book [John Witherow and Patrick Bishop, The Winter War (London: Quartet Books, 1982)], are taken from this interview.

8. Henry James, National Association of Pension Funds, London, England. Interview with the author, 7 September 1983. All subsequent remarks by Mr. James are taken from this interview.

9. The officials who espoused these opinions to the author during private interviews prefer to remain anonymous.

10. Defence Committee, "The Handling of Press," p xxiii.

11. The official who espoused this opinion to the author during a private interview prefers to remain anonymous.

12. Brian Hanrahan and Robert Fox, I Counted Them All Out and I Counted Them All Back (London: British Broadcasting Corporation, 1982), p 117.

13. Alexander Cockburn, "Fact Shortage No Problem, Analysts Say," Harpers (Vol 265, No 1586, July 1982), p 27.

14. John Underwood, Independent Television News, London, England. Interview with the author, 6 September 1983. All subsequent remarks by Mr. Underwood are taken from this interview.

15. Daily Mirror (13 May 1982), p 13.

16. Max Hastings and Simon Jenkins, The Battle for the Falklands (London: Michael Joseph, 1983), p 332.

17. The official who espoused this opinion to the author during a private interview prefers to remain anonymous.

18. Bishop and Witherow, The Winter War, p 150.

19. Defence Committee, "The Handling of Press," p xlvii.

20. Harris, Gotcha!, p 31.

21. Hastings and Jenkins, The Battle for the Falklands, p 159.

22. Ibid., p 331.

23. Defence Committee, "The Handling of Press," p xli.

24. Ibid., p xxxix.

25. Defence Committee, "The Handling of Press," p xl.

26. The officials who espoused these opinions to the author during private interviews prefer to remain anonymous.

27. Sunday Times Insight Team, The Falklands War (London: Sphere Books Limited, 1982), p 212.

28. Geoffrey Archer, "Evidence to the Defence Committee" (Letter written July 1982), p 2.

29. Hanrahan and Fox, I Counted Them All Out, p 109.

30. The official who espoused this opinion to the author during a private interview prefers to remain anonymous.

31. Harris, <u>Gotcha!</u>, p 105.

32. Hastings and Jenkins, <u>The Battle for the Falklands</u>, p 332.

33. Richard Simons and Michael Green, memorandum to David Nicholas (Independent Television News, London, England, July 1982), p 1.

34. Ibid., p 5.

35. Archer, "Evidence to the Defence Committee," p 1.

36. Anthony Holden, <u>Daily Express</u>, London, England. Interview with the author, 10 September 1983. All subsequent comments by Mr. Holden are taken from this interview.

37. Anthony Barnett, <u>New Left Review</u>, London, England. Letter to the author, December 1983.

38. "Falkland Sound/Voces de Malvinas," at the Royal Court Theatre, Summer 1983.

39. Defence Committee, "The Handling of Press," p xxxi.

40. Simons and Green, memorandum, p 4.

41. Defence Committee, "The Handling of Press," p xxxviii.

42. Glasgow Media Group, "War and Peace" (Report issued by the Department of Sociology, University of Glasgow, 1982), p 20.

43. Defence Committee, "The Handling of Press," p xlix.

44. Harris, <u>Gotcha!</u>, p 71.

45. Ibid., p 31.

46. Ibid., p 77.

47. Hastings and Jenkins, <u>The Battle for the Falklands</u>, p 332.

48. The <u>Times</u> (London, May 1982), p 5.

49. Harris, <u>Gotcha!</u>, p 85.

48

50. Ibid., p 91.

51. The Daily Mirror (London, 15 May 1982), p 1; Sunday Times Insight Team, The Falklands War, p 214; Harris, Gotcha!, p 85.

52. The Times (London, 11 May 1982), p 6.

53. Harris, Gotcha!, pp 41–43.

54. Simon Jenkins, "When Soldiers Play Journalist and Journalists Play At Soldiers," Times (London, 10 May 1982), p 8.

55. Anthony Barnett, Iron Britannia (London: Allison and Busby, 1982), p 95.

56. Ibid., p 101.

57. Jerry Adler, "In War, Truth or Faction?", Newsweek (Vol XCIX, No 24, 24 May 1982), p 86.

58. Cockburn, "Fact Shortage No Problem," p 27.

59. Anthony Barnett, "Getting It Wrong and Making It Right," New Socialist (No 13, September/October 1983), p 47.

60. For figures concerning circulation increases, see Anthony Holden, "Fleet Street's War," New Republic (Vol 187, 5 July 1982), p 17.

61. "We Like It So Far," p 27.

62. "Satisfaction Peaks," Economist (Vol 283, No 7236. 8 May 1982), p 25.

63. "End of War," Economist (Vol 283, No 7243, 26 June 1982), p 64.

64. Barnett, Iron Britannia, p 97.

65. Hastings and Jenkins, The Battle for the Falklands, p 135.

66. "The Problems of Peace," Economist (Vol 283, No 7242, 19 June 1982), p 53.

67. Cockburn, "Fact Shortage No Problem," p 27.

68. Hastings and Jenkins, <u>The</u> <u>Battle</u> <u>for</u> <u>the</u> <u>Falklands</u>, p 311.

3

Press-Government Relations
in the United States:
The Iranian Hostage Crisis

At first glance, the 444-day captivity of United States citizens in Iran appears to have little in common with the Argentine military occupation of the Falkland Islands. A 15-month embassy siege differs markedly from an eight-week military engagement. And in Iran, the aggressors controlled communications facilities, so the United States government did not enjoy the practical ability to influence dispatches at the source.

Upon closer examination, however, the parallels between the two crises become evident. Like the Falklands, Iran was a geographical location with which journalists had little familiarity and no expertise. The correspondents dispatched to Tehran spoke no Persian,[1] and consequently — like the British journalists who sailed with the task force — they found themselves at the mercy of people who were both hostile and incomprehensible. In the United States, as in Britain, reporters were kept in the dark or led down the garden path by government officials. Nevertheless, the crisis received heavy exposure, and staunch patriotism in the press contributed to an astounding upsurge of nationalism among the American people.

These circumstantial similarities provide the basis for analysis of the fundamental differences that characterize relations between government and the press in the United States and Britain. Throughout the hostage affair, newspapers managed simultaneously to support the American cause and to criticize the Administration severely. At the same time, journalists in the United States enjoyed their usual ease of access to high-ranking officials, and in fact were regarded as makeshift mediators between Iran and America when normal diplomatic channels failed.

Before embarking on a consideration of the interaction between press and government in the United States during the Iranian hostage crisis, it is worthwhile to examine the general context within which this interaction occurred. Since the 1970's, when America was rocked first by domestic opposition to the Vietnam War and then by the Watergate scandal, relations between press and state were characterized by mutual wariness. During the conflict in Vietnam, television's graphic depiction of the horrors of war, combined with leading newspapers' editorial opposition to the military effort, made the war immensely unpopular among more than half of the United States public and prompted American withdrawal from Indochina. As United States troops left Vietnam, the investigative work of two <u>Washington Post</u> reporters launched the Watergate scandal, which resulted in the resignation of President Nixon. The press derived two lessons from the experience of Vietnam and Watergate: first, that government is susceptible to error and dishonesty; and second, that the media wield enormous power. For its part, the state learned that journalists could be mighty enemies. As a result, relations between government and the press in the United States have been strained since the mid-1970s.

JOURNALISTS IN IRAN

In 1978, popular opposition to Iranian Shah Mohammed Rehza Pahlevi erupted in revolution after two decades of the monarch's repressive, autocratic rule. Correspondents assigned to cover the uprising labored under the handicap of complete unfamiliarity with the nation. No United States newspaper, newsmagazine, or television network maintained a permanent Tehran bureau, and as a result the press lacked understanding and knowledge of the country's culture and politics.[2] For decades coverage of the Shah had been highly favorable, because journalists were not on the scene to recognize popular opposition and the ruler effectively prevented news of such opposition from leaving Iran. As a consequence, when revolution erupted in 1978 the press failed to interpret it correctly. As one commentator remarked early in 1979,

the American news media routinely have characterized the Iranian conflict as the work of turbaned religious zealots in league with opportunistic Marxists, rather than — as they might have — the reaction of people outraged by a repressive regime.
The press, for all its interest in the gold-

rush aspects of Iran's economy, failed to question
the appropriateness of the Shah's version of
economic development and to question his asser-
tions that major parts of the program had been a
success....The belief that the Shah had widespread
popular support went unquestioned until the scale
of the 1978 demonstrations, general strikes, and
labor stoppages made it impossible to sustain.[3]

In 1979, finally, the American media realized that they had
been deluded about events in Iran.
    This realization prompted editors to improve on past
performance by ceasing to rely exclusively on United States
government intelligence concerning Iran. American officials
had been hoodwinked by the Shah, and without any intention
of misleading the media they had called all the shots wrong.
As late as the fall of 1979, every American adviser except
National Security Council Iran expert Gary Sick was predict-
ing political continuity in Iran. Once the inevitability of the
Shah's demise became apparent, United States policy flip-
flopped with seeming disregard for the consequences. Am-
bassador William Sullivan convinced the Carter Administration
that American interests would not be injured significantly if
the Shah abdicated in favor of a revolutionary leader; as a
result, the United States decided to support the Shah's
departure and the formation of a civilian government under
National Front leader Shahpur Bakhtiar.[4]
    Clearly, then, official American reports could not be
trusted, and newspapers began sending in correspondents to
cover the revolution. Nevertheless, by November of 1979,
when the hostages were seized, journalists had been in Iran
for less than a year. They were sufficiently ill-informed
about the country and its civil war to treat the embassy
takeover lightheartedly, as an exciting interlude in a
generally incomprehensible domestic upheaval. One group of
correspondents organized a betting pool and invited wagers on
the hostages' release date.[5] Overjoyed by the warm recep-
tion suddenly accorded reporters after months of hostility and
evasiveness, American correspondents responded eagerly to
Iranian efforts to publicize the embassy seizure. "The
Iranians committed an act of war against the United States
— and then invited the American media, print and electronic,
to cover the story."[6]
    Indeed, the militants who surrounded the embassy were
so acutely aware of the persuasive powers of the media that
they saved their belligerent displays of anti-United States
fervor for the television cameras, prompting former National

Security Adviser Zbigniew Brzezinski to speak bitterly of "those daily shows from the embassy that the Iranians were only too happy to put on."[7] Even more impressive, demonstrators gave interviews selectively, snubbing PBS's "MacNeil-Lehrer Report" to court the higher ratings of CBS's "60 Minutes."[8] At the close of the crisis, on 29 December 1980, William Safire noted in the New York Times that Iran was attempting cleverly to wring American hearts, and thus to improve the Iranian bargaining position, by permitting the networks to film the hostages suffering through their second Christmas in captivity (p A19).

Reporters responded ambivalently to such clever attempts to control access to information. As former Washington Post Tehran correspondent Stuart Auerbach states, "Sure, they attempted to use us, attempted to manipulate us."[9] At the same time, he recalls, he debated the validity of Iranian claims at length in serious discussions with militants who were westernized as well as deeply religious and revolutionary.

> It's a very odd situation to be in a country which is all but at war with your country, and yet to eat in local restaurants and shop in the native bazaars and see people in the streets smoking Marlboro cigarettes, selling models of PanAm jets and Goodyear blimps, and carrying suitcases printed to look like the American flag.

All journalists love a colorful story, and Iranian willingness to permit press coverage of the embassy occupation created a field day for the American media.

Nevertheless, the field day was shortlived: in January of 1980 Iran resumed its usual attitude of hostility toward the press. Throughout the previous two months, since the beginning of the crisis, reporters had recognized the shortcomings of working in a country with a long tradition of censorship. The national government was neither accustomed nor receptive to journalistic scrutiny, and local media were strictly controlled. Moreover, correspondents rarely enjoyed access to the incarcerated hostages. In January, the inherent tension between Iranian militants and American reporters came to a head when journalists were expelled from the country.

The ouster of reporters occurred for several reasons. Paramount among these was the American failure to report events as Iran wanted. By permitting journalists access to the embassy compound and to the militants, the Iranian government genuinely had hoped to prove to the American people that national outrage in Iran was profound and legitimate. When no United States apologies or concessions emerged, Tehran was forced to recognize the failure of its strategy. From this admission stemmed the concomitant belief that — just as the Iranian press supported the existing regime, first under the Shah and then under Khomeini — American journalists were pawns of the United States government and ought to be expelled as representatives of a hated nation.[10]

A second set of reasons for the expulsion of American journalists concerned Iranian fears that the press was having a deleterious effect on factious domestic events. In particular, the regime feared that uprisings among the Kurdish and Azerbaijani minorities were being fuelled by extensive press coverage. By removing the publicity for these uprisings, Iran expected to sap their strength.[11] At the same time, the Revolutionary Council hoped to reduce the political clout of the student militants, who had begun to seem disproportionately powerful, by barring access to their media lifeline.[12] In addition to being disapppointed with the inability of journalists to cause a change of heart in the United States, then, Iran resented the divisive domestic effects of publicity.

Even after American journalists had been evicted, schisms in Iranian politics permitted the circumvention of strict expulsion orders. As Auerbach explains, "When everybody got kicked out, that was the ascendancy of the Beards over the Neckties," of the revolutionary radicals over the westernized moderates in government. During the ten-week expulsion period, however, each of the three American television networks maintained an international crew in Tehran, living in their usual hotel suites and using their customary equipment, which was never evacuated. The Neckties managed to ensure that the journalists could stay, explains Auerbach,

> because — and this is just my impression — they wanted an opening to the West. We were a channel of communication; in the early days we had been a channel of their views.

The Beards were aware of the continued presence of the network reporters, and published diatribes against both journalists and Neckties in local Iranian newspapers, but the correspondents remained in Tehran.

JOURNALISTS IN THE UNITED STATES

News Management by Government

Meanwhile, in the United States officials attempted through news management to counter the publicity advantage enjoyed by Iran as a result of the militants' intensive access to the media. Usually, Administration efforts to mislead the press resulted not from a desire for good publicity but from the hopes of avoiding an irrevocable confrontation with Iran. In attempting to keep open potential channels of negotiation and compromise, the United States faced the problem of

> a classic difference in perspective between jour-
> nalists and diplomats. State department officials
> and diplomats are primarily interested in keeping
> relations with another country fluid, even
> ambiguous, so as to keep the lines open for
> negotiation. Journalists, on the other hand, tend
> to ask questions for the record, in an attempt to
> eliminate ambiguities, and which might make bar-
> gaining more difficult. U.S. officials were upset,
> for instance, when reporters asked Iranians on
> television if executions were possible or likely.[13]

Former White House press secretary Jody Powell believes that government is justified in lying about its activities because of the twin, often mutually contradictory, rights of the state to maintain some secrecy about sensitive matters and of newspapers to publish all available information.[14]
Thus when the United States first learned of the embassy seizure, the Administration used the press to emphasize commitment to a policy of patient restraint while secretly preparing contingency military plans. Powell explains, "We wanted to avoid doing anything that might provoke a violent and irreconcilable response on their part."[15] By the same token, plans for the Shah's departure from Texas in January of 1980 were not revealed until the last minute in order to prevent an outburst of rage from Iran.[16] And during secret negotiations with Iranian counsel Bourget and Villalon, the Administration sidestepped journalists' queries concerning Bani-Sadr's oblique references to private peace talks.

> We had to convey the idea that the Administration
> was doing something behind the scenes, without in
> any way compromising our plan...Bani-Sadr [was]
> saying that the Ayatollah had apporoved a "secret

plan" for the release of the hostages. After several months of nothing but harsh rhetoric coming out of Tehran, the American press had worked itself into a frenzy trying to find out what was going on.[17]

Thus the government managed the press in order to ensure the fruitful progress of negotiations between the United States and Iran.

Occasionally false stories were circulated in the press for reasons unconnected with the sanctity of delicate political maneuvers. French lawyer Nuri Albala, former Amnesty International chief Sean MacBride, and Benin University Law School dean Robert Dossou all floated fictitious reports of an international inquiry into the Shah's crimes in the hopes of involving United Nations Secretary General Kurt Waldheim in efforts to free the hostages.[18] The strategy worked, and in January of 1980 Waldheim travelled to Iran, seeking through his eminent international standing to extract some concessions from the militants. On 31 December 1979, William Safire referred in his New York Times column to an internal White House memorandum urging President Carter to participate in the debate preceding the Iowa Democratic caucus. Safire charged that this memo, complete with Carter's scrawled rejection of his aides' advice, was circulated by Jody Powell in a deliberate attempt to evoke favorable publicity for the President.

> Since Mr. Powell does not usually leak to all and sundry such confidential advice to his boss, the information is necessarily suspect — indeed, those cushion-shot press releases are usually the opposite of the truth....The President is better off running against Khomeini and Ghotbzadeh than Kennedy and Brown, which is why — for the first time — Mr. Carter finds the White House a refuge instead of a trap. (p A15)

Seven months later, Times columnist James Reston underscored Safire's message, pointing out on 30 July 1980 that the President

> didn't really "run" in the primaries at all. He stayed in the White House. He didn't run against Kennedy, but against Ayatollah Khomeini. His argument was that he was struggling for the honor of the nation and that a vote for Kennedy or

> anybody else was a vote against the President's ef-
> forts to liberate the hostages. (p A21)

News management, then, was deployed to convey various
desired messages: in the one case, to Kurt Waldheim; and in
the other, to the voting public.

News Management and the Rescue Mission

The Administration's attempt to shape press coverage
in connection with the April 1980 rescue mission is particularly interesting because it provides a simultaneous example of efforts to maintain absolute secrecy during the
planning stages of a sensitive maneuver and, later, to minimize public perception that a blunder had been committed.
Because complete advance secrecy about the mission was vi-
tal to its success, Powell recalls, until the last minute
"statements were made, both on the record and in background briefings, from the level of the President on down,"
that military intervention might occur in the distant future
but would not involve a direct strike on Tehran.
Government attempts to minimize the diplomatic
damage done by the mission's miscarriage were somewhat
less successful. Newsday reporter Susan Page comments that
"The Carter Administration was not so adept at damage control, backing up off a story, getting away from it."[19] The
Administration's strategy for downplaying the failure of the
rescue attempt involved convincing the American public that
military action, although apparently fruitless, actually had ac-
complished important general aims. By describing the crisis
as more manageable after the mission, the President tried
simultaneously to diminish his own failure and to free himself for electoral campaigning. On May 2, New York Times
columnist Tom Wicker noted this strategy and asserted that
"Carter is not showing much of the candor and honesty with
which primary voters have been crediting him." (p A27)
On the same day, the Washington Post editorialized that "the
president's explanation of why he now feels free to break
out of the White House...is unreal and implausible and unper-
suasive." (p A16) Similarly, New Yorker magazine noted on
June 2 that after the rescue mission

> the President made his imcomprehensible state-
> ment that world affairs had become more "manage-
> able" after the failed mission, thus freeing
> him from his vow to stick to business in the

White House and refrain from campaigning for
reelection as long as the hostages were being held
in Iran.[20]

Thus journalists were not fooled by Carter's attempt simultaneously to downplay the rescue mission's failure and to ex-
tricate himself from his politically disadvantageous seclusion
in the White House.

Media awareness of such news management notwithstanding, in general the press complied with Carter's
novel attempt to behave as if the situation in Tehran had
improved. The New Yorker commented that

> Since the disastrous mission to release the
> American hostages in Iran, coverage of the
> hostages, which once blanked the news columns
> and the airwaves to the exclusion of any other
> news, has evaporated...The news organizations,
> which so often follow the President's lead, fell in
> step with him this time, too, and inaugurated their
> policy of ignoring the hostages....the average wat-
> cher of the news, who at one moment was invited
> to occupy his thoughts with nothing but the
> hostages and the next moment was asked to forget
> all about them, is left with a feeling that he has
> been used.[21]

To the extent that media coverage of the hostage crisis
slackened after the rescue mission, the Administration
succeeded in its efforts to make bad news palatable.

It is not certain, however, that news coverage of the
hostages decreased solely as the result of government news
management. Jody Powell claims that "there were a whole
lot of things going on in the country before then that we
were trying to get coverage for," without much success.
The inability of the Administration to publicize the windfall
profits tax, for example, indicates that the media pursued
the hostage story regardless of White House efforts to steer
the news in other directions.

Since press coverage of the crisis did decrease after
the rescue mission failed, though, some explanation of the
change is necessary. First, and most important, reporters
were expelled from Iran once again, and consequently access
to stories was limited. Then, too, the media

may have been responding to public fatigue with
the issue as well as to Presidential wishes.   In
recent times, there has been a tendency for a
single issue to dominate the news for a period
and then suddenly drop from sight, in obedience
to a rhythm of public attention which seems to
belong more in the world of entertainment than
in the world of international affairs.[22]

Certainly nothing of any interest or significance was happen-
ing in Iran during the weeks immediately following the
rescue mission.
    To ignore the impact on the press of the
Administration's decision to de-emphasize the hostage crisis
would be foolish, however.   Other factors may have influenced the news slowdown, but presidential power to shape
the news extends beyond deliberate attempts at news
management.   When Carter was preoccupied with the
hostages his concern was translated into extensive media
coverage, and when he recommenced campaigning the press
began reporting on his politicking so the hostage crisis
received less exposure.

Self-Restraint by Journalists

    At the same time, news management during the
Iranian crisis was relatively easy because national upheavals
awaken journalists' patriotic sentiments.   As loyal citizens,
reporters are reluctant to risk damaging their country's interests.   In addition, situations involving hostages are treated
with particular sensitivity by the media in order to avoid
angering the captors.   Thus the press initially was highly
receptive to requests by the United States government to
exercise caution in its coverage of the Iranian hostage crisis.
Newspapers refrained from printing stories which vilified the
Shah and thus undermined the unity of the American official
position.[23]   By the same token, seeking to avoid arousing
the Iranian militants, the press tried not to inflame the
American public, and outbursts of patriotic anger in the
United States received minimal media attention.[24]   As
Powell comments,

    I think the press was generally sympathetic,
    and I say this with regard to reporters and to
    commentators,   at the   outset,   to   the
    administration's   policy   of   restraint,   of   not

> doing anything rash...at the beginning some
> of the reporting was quite good...particularly
> out of the Pentagon, was quite helpful in ex-
> plaining why we couldn't just hop over there
> and get those people out.

The press was not averse, then, to following Administration directives concerning coverage of the hostage crisis.

Indeed, journalists joined government officials in calling for self-restraint. With a considerable degree of hesitation, former Undersecretary of State for Iranian Affairs Harold Saunders suggests that

> It's very hard to ask them to do this — it
> runs counter to at least two traditions —
> but I think the media might be asked to help the
> president put things in perspective.[25]

Far from disagreeing with Saunders' request, journalists applauded it. In the New York Times of 3 December 1979, Anthony Lewis anticipated Saunders' suggestion by four years.

> Under our system television networks cannot be
> told to cut out provocative stories, but broad-
> cast executives might begin to ask themselves
> whether they are serving the news or the Ayatol-
> lah by dramatizing "Day 29" and running the mob
> scene nightly. (p A25)

Although Lewis was directly addressing only television journalism, the implications of his comment for the print media are clear, particularly since — as will be seen below — newspapers were equally as guilty as television networks of overplaying the hostage issue. Thus reporters agreed explicitly with the notion that the media should exercise self-restraint in covering the hostage crisis.

It is hardly surprising, therefore, that journalists refrained from printing a number of stories which might have injured the hostages. Virtually every correspondent based in Tehran knew that some embassy officials had escaped capture in the initial melee and were hiding in the city, but not a single journalist reported their existence. Elaine Sciolino, former Newsweek Tehran correspondent, explains that "It was an example of self-censorship in the good sense. It would have been two paragraphs in Newsweek, and these people would have been in physical danger."[26] Ultimately, the six Americans escaped Iran by posing as Canadian businessmen.

By the same token, Sciolino recalls when one hostage "flipped out" and attempted suicide twice, Tehran correspondents kept the matter quiet in order to avoid ruining the captive's future career.

The media also cooperated with specific government attempts to keep open channels of negotiation with Iran. In February of 1980, after receiving a personal request from Carter aide Hamilton Jordan not to report on the Administration's secret negotiations with Iranian lawyers Bourget and Villalon, Katherine Graham ordered both of her major publications, Newsweek and the Washington Post to suppress the story.[27] Toward the end of March 1980, President Carter personally informed a few key newsmen of Iran's offer to transfer custody of the hostages from the militants surrounding the embassy to the Iranian government. Such inside knowledge entailed some liability: Carter asked the journalists not to publicize the Iranian initiative until negotiations seemed secure.[28] By affording several privileged reporters access to secret information, the President bought their silence.

Media willingness to cooperate with government requests for secrecy incurred serious criticism in some quarters. The Nation magazine editorialized on 26 January 1980 that "the media appear to have abandoned all critical scrutiny of the Administration's decision-making process."[29] Referring in particular to United States rejection of an Iranian proposal which was contingent on American recognition of the validity of Iran's grievances, the Nation queried,

> Shouldn't the press report on behind-the-scenes opposition to an important policy decision? Shouldn't the press ask whether any officials in the State Department or the White House favored a more serious weighing of the new Iranian initiative? Instead, our editorial writers have blandly accepted Carter's consistent policy of ruling out any solution involving an investigation of the Iranian grievances against the Shah and the United States prior to release of the hostages.[30]

In pandering to Administration concepts of right and wrong, such reproofs implied, the media abdicated their responsibility to inform the American public fully about developments in Iran and within the United States.

Such allegations seem largely unjustified, because the media never knowingly followed government directives without careful consideration, and in several cases Administration requests for secrecy were denied. The President and many of his advisers were infuriated when NBC negotiated a deal with the militants whereby an interview with hostage William Gallegos was aired on the condition that the Iranian students could present their claims.[31] Four years later, Brzezinski still refers to the NBC interview as "an instance of an American network collaborating with unfriendly interests, with kidnappers." In similarly strong terms, Saunders denounces the interview as "a blatant case of Iranian manipulation of the United States media." Harsh criticism by the government, and the implied demand for future restraint, were met with no sympathy in the press. On 13 December 1979 the Washington Post editorialized that "the press should not be expected to conduct some kind of propaganda control on its coverage." (p A18)

Early in March of 1980, the New York Times reported that high-ranking White House officials personally requested CBS executives to delete a portion of the "60 Minutes" news program which dealt with American relations with the Shah and with the activities of SAVAK (the Shah's secret police). This attempt to suppress the news was flatly rejected by the television networks.[32] By the same token, when Saunders requested Newsweek not to print a cover story providing the names and photographs of all 50 hostages, because some of the captives were concealing CIA involvement by using aliases, "the magazine pretty much told me to shove it."

After the rescue mission failed, the President's suggestion that American journalists leave Iran to avoid injury at the hands of infuriated militants was coldly received. Jody Powell recalls that "the President's first inclination was to get the news organizations to pull their people out." After being reminded that a direct order would arouse charges of news management, Carter merely advised reporters to quit Tehran. As Powell comments, "Probably a few more went in, a few came out. It didn't really make any difference one way or another."

In trying to manage the news or to solicit cooperative self-restraint from journalists, government in America must proceed with caution. Powell points out that heavy reliance on the refuge of designating materials as Classified damages relations between press and the state to the detriment of both. Unless an administration can furnish a specific, convincing reason for requesting that a story be withheld, it relies on the general credibility it has accumulated through years of association with journalists and editors.[33] When this credibility is minimal, government demands for media self-restraint are seldom met and always resented.

Jimmy Carter and the Press

President Carter found himself in a situation of minimal credibility when he entered office. To some extent, press criticism may be the unavoidable legacy of American history. Certainly relations between government and journalists have altered substantially during the past 20 years. Tom Wicker comments that a former Congressman who habitually lay drunk on the floor of the Senate was never exposed because "in the old days it used to be almost a conviction in the press that you protected public officials from that sort of thing, you know, [their own] human frailties and all that."[34] Today, a new generation of journalists has inherited the skepticism born of Vietnam and Watergate. However, journalists are motivated primarily not by an inherent dislike of the Chief Executive but rather by the earnest desire to track the truth despite pressure on all sides. As Tom Wicker comments.

> You're constantly kind of caught between the peace movement, which feels that the press is the handmaiden of government, and the right wing, which says, "Oh God, the press is undermining the government."

Whether or not the press entertains an unshakeable dislike for presidents in general, it is undeniable that Carter received a great deal of bad publicity. For one thing, he was an unfamiliar face in the close-knit, exclusive world of Washington politics. As Newsday correspondent Susan Page recalls, "When Carter came into the White House a lot of reporters sort of said, 'Who is this guy?', like he didn't have any right to be there." Thus Carter entered office at a disadvantage.

Nor did he win the admiration of journalists by failing to be friendly and by claiming as justification for his aloofness that he was too righteous to engage in politicking and currying favor. Tom Wicker explains, "He alienated people from the start by being holier-than-thou: 'I'll never tell you a lie' and all that junk." Because of his deeply moral stance, Carter failed to fit in with Washington's leaders, particularly in the media. A newcomer to Washington and its ways, Carter was lambasted in the press for both his inexperience and his diffidence.

Despite journalists' dislike of Carter, the early stages of the hostage crisis witnessed some support for his efforts to deal with Iran. Throughout November, people stirred by patriotism looked to the Chief Executive as the symbol of their beloved country; only later did the hostages' continued captivity prompt charges of Presidential weakness. On 9 November 1979 James Reston wrote in the New York Times that Carter "has been leading us through the latest Iranian crisis with admirable restraint, and deserves the patience and support of the nation." (p A35) Four days later, the Times editorialized that

> President Carter is being both wise and firm in his contest against Ayatollah Khomeini... The President has skirted the twin dangers of inaction and over-reaction. He deserves admiration and support. (p A22)

On November 14, the Washington Post applauded the President's move to embargo Iranian oil (p A26). On the 22nd, Anthony Lewis praised Carter in the Times for moving the American fleet in the Middle East closer to Iran (pA23).

However, as the embassy siege dragged on, the initial burst of enthusiasm for Carter waned rapidly, and he returned to his usual lowly place in journalistic esteem. Indeed, during the crisis he was particularly harshly treated, because by criticizing the President the press could vent its general frustration at being confronted with a problem which could not rightfully be attributed to any American politician. Jody Powell recalls that it was impossible for government officials, much less for the media, to interpret events in revolutionary Iran "with perfect lucidity." Unable to believe that a reliable Iranian negotiator could not be located and that therefore Carter was reduced to flailing at straw men, journalists faulted the President for the hostages' continued captivity. In the New York Times of 17 December 1979 William Safire ironically posed a series of rhetorical questions.

> Did the United States respond to an act of war promptly and effectively? As a result of the Carter response, are terrorists in Iran and elsewhere in the world less likely to use kidnapping against Americans as a tool to gain attention and influence policy? Did the United States gain or lose respect among nations who depend on our resolve for protection? Has our extended patience made our nuclear deterrent more or less credible? (p A27)

On 13 March 1980 Joseph Kraft of the <u>Washington</u> <u>Post</u> specifically addressed Carter's claim that his hands were tied by the absence of a reliable decisionmaker in Iran:

> The con game consists of the notion — sedulously cultivated by the White House and the State Department flacks — that Iran is run by a bunch of crazy weirdos capable of doing anything at any time. Matters are so delicate, the argument goes, that only the president can manage the affair. To criticize Carter on Iran is to seem to be playing fast and loose with the lives of innocent Americans.
>
> The Iranian political situation in fact is not a mad scene. If nothing else, there is a clear top man. Ayatollah Khomeini, and he alone, has the power to loose the hostages. (p A19)

Thus anger at the President's inability to free the hostages was accentuated by the conviction that his lamentations about Iranian unreliability were mere political hokum.

As the crisis continued, Brzezinski notes, the attitude of the press toward Carter "was developing adversarily." Former Secretary of State Cyrus Vance recalls that journalists "basically were more biased at the end against the Carter Administration."[35]

One misunderstanding in particular strained relations between reporters and the Administration. Just before the Wisconsin primary, an official statement from Bani-Sadr was expected concerning the possibility that custody of the hostages would be transferred from the militants to the Iranian Parliament. Upon receiving the statement at 4:00 am on April 1, the Administration privately alerted representatives of the country's major news organizations that a breakthrough was imminent. The President then won the Wisconsin primary that day, and when Iran reneged on the offer to transfer custody, he was accused of lying to better his electoral chances.[36]

Powell argues that Carter's positive response to Bani-Sadr was not prompted by hopes of winning the primary.

> By that weekend it was clear that we had the thing won...If it had been held on Saturday we would have beaten them by at least as much as we did. Anyway, Wisconsin is not New York.

Whether or not the Administration deliberately misled the press — and there is no reason to believe that it did, since it merely responded enthusiastically to a proposition whose later retraction could not have been foreseen —journalists felt used.

Criticism of Carter in the press intensified noticeably throughout April and subsequent months. On the 10th, George F. Will castigated the President in the Washington Post for showing neither initiative nor resolve in his dealings with Iran. (p A15) On the 16th, New York Times columnist James Reston noted that Carter's "patience has begun to be regarded as impotence." (p A27) On April 25, the Washington Post editorialized that Carter must "suggest to the Iranians that the price of keeping the hostages is going to get — and quickly — unacceptably high." (p A14) On May 22, William Safire of the Times advised the President to stop waffling and "declare economic warfare on Iran." (p A35)

When he did take decisive action, Carter received no thanks from the press. On April 9, Reston registered disapproval of new economic sanctions against Iran — "as for the hostages, it is hard to believe them safer or closer to liberation than they were last week" (p A27) — and on the 25th he decried Carter's threats to use force if the hostages were not released soon (p A27). On June 12, the New York Times editorialized that Carter should not have staked his reputation on prosecuting Ramsey Clark for visiting Tehran despite the existence of a Presidential ban on travel to Iran:

> One of these days, an Iranian government may actually be functioning and asking to deal with a Ramsey Clark or other admirer of the revolution to arrange the hostages' release. When the call comes, would Mr. Carter pardon Mr. Clark or merely parole him from jail? (p A30)

Thus neither attempts at appeasement nor efforts to take a tough stance met with approval in the press.

Noting the fact that Carter could do no good in the eyes of journalists, Brzezinski states that some reporters "don't have much constancy in the way they operate." Lacking basic opinions or political orientation, such columnists criticize the government regardless of the policies it pursues and the initiatives it takes. For his part, Jody Powell confesses to a particular dislike of Washingon Post columnists Rowland Evans and Robert Novak, whose reporting style earned them the nickname "Errors and No Facts" from the Carter Administration.[37]

68

The Administration and the Press

If the press was hostile to Carter, it showed little
more regard for key officials in his administration. Indeed,
it publicized their disagreements in a manner that made
Cabinet members appear no better than fishwives haggling at
market. Journalists inplicitly tend to subscribe to theorist
Graham Allison's model of public policy as the outcome of
bureaucratic conflict. Dissension is easier to describe, and
infinitely more likely to attract reader interest, than ac-
counts of the slow, reflective thought processes that constitute the real basis of policy.

Thus journalists spotlighted disagreements between
Brzezinski and Vance.[38] Basically, the difference of opinion
regarding Iran was one of orientation. After the revolution
began but before the hostages were seized, Brzezinski was
preoccupied with Iran only insofar as the country affected
American interests in the oil-rich Persian Gulf area. Vance,
by contrast, was specifically concerned to promote
democratization in Iran. Once the hostages were taken,
Vance's primary goal was to free them, whereas Brzezinski
addressed the general problem of deteriorating relations between the United States and Iran.

Then, too, Brzezinski's tendency to assume center
stage irritated Vance. Although Vance did not enjoy briefing
the press to clarify the American position on international
issues, he resented the National Security Adviser's assumption
of a function which traditionally is performed by the
Secretary of State. Even when Brzezinski responded to a
spate of serious attacks in the press by announcing a decision to tone down his public image, he kept a finger in
every pie. Not content with Jody Powell's command of foreign affairs, for example, Brzezinski appointed an Associate
Press Secretary of his own.

Vance, by comparison, liked to maintain a relatively
low profile in the press. During the hostage crisis he
received comparatively little media coverage, except after
the rescue mission, when he was excoriated for resigning and
leaving Carter in the lurch. On April 29, the New York
Times printed an editorial stating that

> it is not enough to jump ship. By doing so, he
> has led the country and the world to believe that
> the United States is committing an intolerable
> strategic error. A lawyer whose advice is
> ignored tells his client to find another attor-
> ney. A defeated statesman speaks his mind. (pA22)

On the same day, the <u>Washington</u> <u>Post</u> editorialized that, although Vance's resignation satisfied his personal scruples, "whether it is understandable in terms of the ethic of public service is another matter. The resignation is a stunning embarrassment to Mr. Carter." (p A16)

Unlike Carter, Brzezinski, and Vance, Jody Powell entered the hostage crisis with sizeable reserves of trust and admiration from the press. In large part, Powell's popularity stemmed from his reliability. Carter writes that

> Only very rarely in the four years was Jody excluded from my discussion of even the most sensitive issues. The reporters understood this special relationship between us and learned to trust the accuracy of his statements and answers.[39]

Although many administrations prefer press secretaries to function as mouthpieces for policies of which they are ignorant, Powell's access to inside information was frequently helpful. Powell asserts,

> You can do a much better job of keeping the secret if you know there's a secret there to be kept ...A lot of that is an art, and you can't expect a robot to perform like an artist. If you treat a press secretary like a robot, he's not going to be able to do anything artistic.

A press secretary with faint, non-specific knowledge of sensitive matters can publicize them unwittingly. Powell comments that "in two or three hours you can get a good portion of the whole goddamn government whispering and asking about what's going on over dinner or afternoon drinks." Far better, he claims, to have full advance knowledge of the tricky issues, because journalists "really can't capture and they can't torture" a press secretary to pick his brain.

However, Powell's privy status had its dark side, because the knowledgeable press secretary often is held accountable for the information he repeats. Particularly when the administration he serves is unpopular, the press secretary incurs a sizeable share of media wrath. When Carter's victory in the April primary was attributed to skillful news management, then, the blame was placed squarely on Powell.[40]

His guilt was assumed more automatically than might have been the case normally, because a few weeks earlier he had been directly involved in an incident which undeniably

had justified allegations of media manipulation by the
government. Iran announced, toward the end of March, that
Carter had written to Khomeini apologizing abjectly for
United States support of the Shah. Powell recalls that
"there had been a letter, but it was a letter of an entirely
different kind": an ultimatum to Bani-Sadr, threatening the
use of force if the hostages were not freed immediately.
When queried by the press about the supposed American
apology, Powell did not mention the real letter for fear of
tipping Bani-Sadr's hand. By denying the alleged letter
without simultaneously revealing the existence of the real
letter, Powell admits,

> I didn't lie to them, but I certainly did mislead
> them...I happened to think at the time, and I still
> think, that it was a legitimate thing for a
> government spokesman to do.

Legitimate or not, Powell's action seriously damaged his
relationship with the press.

NATIONALISM IN THE PRESS

Despite the conflicts and ill will between the Administration and the press, journalists supported the United
States with a patriotic fervor that was highly unusual in the
post-Vietnam, post-Watergate era. Reporters were genuinely
outraged by the idea that innocent American citizens could
be held captive in their own embassy, particularly by a rabid
mob of incomprehensible religious fundamentalists, and their
emotion was reflected in print. Throughout the crisis, even
when journalistic support for Carter and his initiatives was
at its lowest ebb, reporters fulminated against the Iranians.
As one commentator remarked,

> To sift through the immense amount of material
> generated by the U.S. embassy takeover in Tehran
> on November 4, 1979, is to be struck by a number
> of things. First, it seemed that "we" were at
> bay, and with "us" the normal, democratic, rational
> order of things. Out there, writhing in self-
> provoked frenzy, was "Islam" in general, whose
> manifestation then was a disturbingly neurotic
> Iran.[41]

Never once, except in staunchly liberal journals of opinion, was it suggested that Iranian grievances might be legitimate.

Characterization of Khomeini and his followers was unilaterally unfavorable, even vicious. On 6 November 1979 the New York Times editorialized that "In the zealous eyes of Ayatollah Khomeini, America is the 'great satan' and Great Britain its 'evil' ally. But it is the Ayatollah himself who is doing the devil's work." (p A18) On the 27th of the month, a Times editorial highlighted "the difference between an ascetic man of holiness and a primitive man of hate" (p A22) so that the newspaper's readers would understand that Khomeini embodied the latter category. The following day, Meg Greenfield of the Washington Post described events in Iran as "A return to Tribalism." (p A23) On 31 January 1980 a particularly rabid New York Times editorial scoffed at Ghotbzadeh for his anger concerning the escape of the six American officials who posed as Canadians, and reassured readers that future attempts to pronounce the Iranian leader's tongue-twisting name would be unnecessary because "the man himself has now settled beyond reasonable doubt what Americans should call him: muddled, and mean." (p A22) On July 3, a Times editorial gleefully warned Khomeini that his ban on Western music would backfire: "You can't stop popular music any more than you can stop popular political ideas — and...to try is itself a sign of rumbling trouble." (p A18) On the 29th of the month, the Times compared the Shah favorably to the Khomeini regime, claiming that "at least the Shah felt enough shame to insist that torture had been stopped. His successors flaunt their cruelties." (p A14) On December 23, the Washington Post denounced the Iranian offer to exchange the hostages for $24 billion in financial guarantees as "grotesque and offensive." (p A14)

Such overwhelmingly unfavorable coverage of Iran did not occur sporadically; on the contrary, the press hammered home the message relentlessly, prompting some commentators to dub the crisis "a media event." Throughout all 444 days of the hostages' captivity the media treated their incarceration as the most important issue facing the United States. It is estimated that the three major television networks spent a combined total of $1 million daily on crisis coverage.[42]

And television was not alone in hyper-publicizing the issue. On 5 December 1979 the New York Times editorialized, "So long as the hostages sit bound in Teheran, they should be the focus of American concern." (p A30) On the 17th, the Washington Post reiterated the message: "There is something Ghotbzadeh needs desperately to know: the hostages are the only issue." (p A20) The Post's lead editorial on Christmas Day 1979 urged Americans to "think about the hostages today." (p A16) The following day, Meg Greenfield's Post column stated that fair-minded efforts to sympathize with Iranian grievances dangerously obscured the central issue: namely, the seizure of the hostages. (p A15)

The effect of such media hype was profound. In the first place, extensive exposure of the crisis undoubtedly contributed to the patriotism that swept the United States. Once relentless news coverage sanctioned public outrage, nationalist sentiments could be expressed that had long been considered unfashionable.[43] American citizens responded furiously to the embassy seizure, burning Iranian flags, refusing to unload Iranian ships and to refuel Iranian airplanes, and attacking pro-Iranian demonstrations.

To some extent, of course, media emphasis on the crisis followed perceived public interest in the topic. As Wicker points out, "You have to ask 'Why were they [the media] doing it?' Because as newsmen they sensed an intense public interest in it." Former Washington Post Tehran correspondent Cody recalls that

> The situation was like an exposed nerve in the United States. As a result, every small development on the hostages or even indirectly related to them was big news. We therefore sent out reams of copy on every little thing we could find out or that was said about them.[44]

It is hardly surprising that a crisis designated top national priority received a great deal of media attention.

In addition to contributing to public excitement about the crisis, extensive news coverage unwittingly may have aided the Iranian cause. Confidence that the American media would ensure the hostages' continued importance as a bargaining chip permitted the militants, the Revolutionary Council, and later the Iranian Parliament to adopt an intransigent position in negotiations with the United States. As Philip Geyelin wrote in the Washington Post on 13 May 1980,

> The daily drumbeat of American attention, the urgent expressions of official concern, the plain evidence of the high price this country attached to their freedom — all this, the theory goes, was exactly what the Iranian militants wanted. (p A17)

In the words of Brzezinski, Iran "wanted to keep this item on the front burner," and the American press obliged. "Every day the issue was being dramatized and therefore emotionalized by the media," recalls the former National Security Adviser. The New York Times alluded to the potentially harmful effects of such dramatization in a 6 January 1980 editorial concerning the expulsion of American journalists from Tehran: "Without the most intensely interested reporters asking embarrassing questions, it might even be decided one morning that the hostages had already been tried, found guilty and expelled." (p A24) The dilemma faced by journalists was summarized neatly in Ellen Goodman's Washington Post column on 17 June 1980:

> For a long time, journalists had gnawed at the question of whether they were reporting an event or contributing to it. If you cover the event created especially for you, are you being manipulated? If you don't, are you neglecting it? (p A17)

In answer to these questions, New York Times columnist James Reston admits that Iran may have benefited from media emphasis on the crisis, but states that "I don't see what we could do other than publish what was going on."[45]

On the other hand, it is possible that heavy American coverage of the crisis did not affect Iranian attitudes and decisions. Elaine Sciolino, formerly of Newsweek, maintains that "the hostages were released when the Iranians were good and ready to release them. The Waldheim commission, that whole UN baloney, the business with the French lawyers — all that had no effect." Militants and officials in Iran acted upon deeply felt grievances, and media coverage may have been largely incidental to the basic issue of hostility toward the United States. As early as April 1980 it became clear that the hostages would not be freed except by an order of Parliament, which had not yet been elected.[46]

Probably the most important effect of extensive media coverage was the Administration's belief that the public demanded a definitive response to Iranian aggression. In fact, it is likely that Carter decided to attempt the rescue mission largely because of the intensive exposure given the hostages.[47] Particularly in an election year, the pressure generated by public desire for action was enormous. In the wake of the failed rescue effort, journalists began to harbor

> suspicions that their own disproportionate coverage
> of [the crisis], together with the Presidential cam-
> paign, had generated the terrifying vortex of
> political pressure that brought on the tragic rescue
> mission and came near to dragging the nation into
> a catastrophe.[48]

Four years later, the consensus among reporters and
politicians alike is that constant media coverage of the
hostages narrowed the range of options available to the Administration in its attempts to solve the crisis.

Given the profound effect exercised by the media on
public opinion, on events in Iran, and on the American
government, it seems reasonable to describe the press as a
participant in the hostage crisis. Such a description is particularly appropriate in light of the fact that often Iran and
the United States addressed each other only through the
media. On 12 December 1979 the New York Times
editorialized that "in the absence of formal contacts, journalists have become surrogate diplomats." (p A30) One
month later, on January 11, the Washington Post concurred
that "journalists have been the only direct link between the
American public and Iran for more than two months." (pA14)

Sometimes the mediating function of the press extended beyond merely publicizing the initiatives of the adver-
saries, and involved direct assistance to high-ranking government officials in Iran and the United States. On 15 November 1979 Bani-Sadr asked Post correspondent Jonathan Randal
and Los Angeles Times reporter Doyle McManus to his home
to discuss possible solutions to the crisis.[49] By the same
token, one of the Tehran newspaper correspondents travelled
to Washington to brief the Defense Department on events in
Iran.[50] Frequently American officials learned of new
developments on the Iranian side only by reading newspapers
or watching television.[51]

However, because the term "mediator" is highly
specific, some journalists and government officials are reluctant to assign it to the press. Former Washington Post Tehran correspondent Cody reflects that

> Inasmuch as the Iranian and U.S. governments...had
> only fragmentary information about what was going
> on, I suppose you could make a case that demands
> and responses, and certainly attitudes, were passed
> from Tehran to Washington and vice versa through
> the media. But it seems to me that is different
> from mediation.

According to Jody Powell, "that is a role that the media claims for itself, that in some cases may be true," but generally refers only to the fact that the press provides a forum of expression for both parties in a conflict. Brzezinski and Vance categorically deny that the press functioned as an unofficial arbitrator between Iran and the United States. As far as the former National Security Adviser is concerned, journalists have no role in politics beyond the reporting of events.

While agreeing with Brzezinski that the press did not mediate the conflict, Hal Saunders feels differently about the function of the media in general.

> I have a rather broad view of the diplomatic process...In a crisis like this, all the routes of normal diplomacy were shattered by Iran, so what you do is you try to seek the most imaginative channels possible.

One such channel, Saunders suggests, might be a documentary investigating the relationship of the United States to the Shah. "A television executive is an American citizen too," and by producing such a program he might help to ease tensions between America and Iran.

Saunders' proposition raises complex ethical questions for reporters, most of whom believe that they are mandated only to report objectively on events in government. Indeed, few journalists actively sought their role as intermediary in the hostage crisis, and many prominent journalists — Tom Wicker and Drew Middleton among them — regret the integral involvement of the press in the diplomatic process during the hostage crisis. As Elaine Sciolino states, "We are not advisers to our governments. If you want to know what's going on, read what I write in my magazine."

CONCLUSION

The fact that journalists worried about their unintentional participation in the political process during the hostage crisis is equally as interesting, and equally as telling about the role of the press in the United States, as the fact that journalists were able to participate in the first place. The American media occupy a position of importance in society which is unrivalled in any other Western democracy. When the hostages were allowed to send mail home, they wrote to the White House, to their families, to schools whose students

had sent letters — and to the Washington Post.[52]   By the
same token, whereas officials in other countries might have
relied on businessmen to fill the vacuum created by the rup-
ture of normal diplomatic channels, the Carter Administration
turned to the press.

Indeed, it is arguable that the press functioned as the
proverbial "strong man" during the hostage crisis. Far from
following a robust government reaction to the embassy
seizure, the media served to mold and to channel — and, to
a significant extent, to force — Administration initiatives.
From the start, the press carved out for itself a narrow territory between harsh criticism of the government and virulent
support for the American cause.   Only a national press with
little fear of government recrimination can afford to attack
the Chief Executive during time of crisis; to call the media
in the United States fearless is to state a truism.   Journalists in America have ended wars and toppled Presidents,
and they are not bashful about flexing their collective
muscle.

Free to criticize the government, they are also free
to respond on an ad hoc basis to its requests for journalistic
discretion.   Sharing the national sense of anger about the il-
legal attack on the embassy, and wanting to further the negotiation process whereby the hostages might be freed, the
press complied with many Administration attempts to maintain secrecy.   On the other hand, the press frequently
refused to withhold stories, aware that Carter and his advisers could do no more than express displeasure.   When all
three major television networks aired portions of a film
made by the militants, in which the hostages concurred with
Iranian accusations of the United States, the State Department dismissed the film as a "a cynical propaganda ploy, but
did not criticize the networks for presenting it."[53]   In
America, the government has acquired habits of respect
during two centuries of interaction with a national press
which was born in an atmosphere of freedom, constitutionally
mandated to report at will, and accustomed to influence the
decisions of policymakers.

1. Arlie Schardt, "Dateline Tehran," Newsweek (Vol XCIV, No 23, 3 December 1979), p 8753.

2. Barry Rubin, Paved With Good Intentions (New York: Oxford University Press, 1980), p 338.

3. William A. Dorman and Ehsan Omeed, "Reporting Iran the Shah's Way," Columbia Journalism Review (Vol 17, No 5, January/February 1979), p 29.

4. For a discussion of American policy in Iran during late 1979, see Zbigniew Brzezinski, Power and Principle (New York: Farrar Straus Giroux, 1983), pp 359–376.

5. Doyle McManus, Free At Last! (New York: The New American Library, Inc., 1981), p 59.

6. Edwin Diamond, Sign Off (Cambridge MA: The MIT Press, 1982), p 112.

7. Zbigniew Brzezinski, Center for Strategic and International Studies, Washington DC. Telephone conversation with the author, 16 December 1983. All subsequent remarks by Dr. Brzezinski, unless noted as being from his book Power and Principle, are taken from this conversation.

8. Jennifer Parmelee, "From Firemen to Diplomats: The Western Media and Iran Before and After the Revolution" (Near Eastern Studies Senior Thesis, Princeton University, 6 May 1980), p 94.

9. Stuart Auerbach, Washington Post, Washington DC. Telephone conversation with the author, 14 December 1983. All subsequent remarks by Mr. Auerbach are taken from this conversation.

10. Rubin, Paved with Good Intentions, p 341.

11. Ibid., p 341.

12. McManus, Free At Last!, p 91.

13. Parmelee, "From Firemen to Diplomats," p 118.

14. Jody Powell, The Other Side of the Story (New York: William Morrow, 1984).

15. Jody Powell, Powell and Associates, Washington DC. Interview with the author, 21 December 1983. All subsequent remarks by Mr. Powell, unless noted as being from his book The Other Side of the Story, are taken from this interview.

16. Hamilton Jordan, Crisis: The Last Year of the Carter Presidency (New York: G.P. Putnam's Sons, 1982), p 98.

17. Ibid., p 54.

18. Pierre Salinger, America Held Hostage: The Secret Negotiations (Garden City NY: Doubleday & Co., Inc., 1981), pp 117–119.

19. Susan Page, Newsday, Long Island NY. Lecture delivered at Harvard University, 30 November 1983. All subsequent remarks by Ms. Page are taken from this lecture.

20. "Notes and Comment," New Yorker (Vol LVI, No 15, 2 June 1980), p 32.

21. Ibid., p 31.

22. Ibid., p 33.

23. Parmelee, "From Firemen to Diplomats," p 109.

24. Diamond, Sign Off, p 113.

25. Harold Saunders, American Enterprise Institute, Washington DC. Interview with the author, 21 December 1983. All subsequent remarks by Mr. Saunders are taken from this interview.

26. Elaine Sciolino, Newsweek, New York City. Telephone conversation with the author, 12 November 1983. All subsequent remarks by Ms. Sciolino are taken from this conversation.

27. Jordan, Crisis, p 149.

28. Jimmy Carter, Keeping Faith (New York: Bantam Books, 1982), p 502.

29. "Lost Chance?", Nation (Vol 230, No 3, 26 January 1980), p 67.

30. Ibid., p 68.

31. Parmelee, "From Firemen to Diplomats," p 90.

32. Les Brown, "White House Sought to Bar '60 Minutes' Segment," New York Times 7 March 1980, p A11.

33. Powell, The Other Side of the Story.

34. Tom Wicker, New York Times, New York City. Interview with the author, 15 December 1983. All subsequent remarks by Mr. Wicker, unless noted as being from his Times column, are taken from this interview.

35. Cyrus Vance, Simpson Thacher and Bartlett, New York City. Interview with the author, 15 December 1983. All subsequent remarks by Mr. Vance are taken from this interview.

36. McManus, Free At Last!, p 135.

37. Powell, The Other Side of the Story.

38. The subsequent discussion of these disagreements is taken from Brzezinski, Power and Principle, pp 30–4–; and from Carter, Keeping Faith, p 54.

39. Carter, Keeping Faith, p 44.

40. The subsequent discussion of journalists' anger with Powell is taken from Powell, The Other Side of the Story; from Jordan, Crisis, p 241; and from Powell's interview with the author.

41. Edward W. Said, "Hiding Islam," Harpers (Vol 262, No 1568, January 1981), p 27.

42. Ibid., p 29.

43. Diamond, Sign Off, p 127.

44. Edward Cody, Washington Post, Washington DC. Letter to the author, December 1983. All subsequent remarks by Mr. Cody are taken from this letter.

45. James Reston, New York Times, New York City. Telephone conversation with the author, 17 November 1983.

46. Cyrus Vance, interview with the author.

47. Diamond, Sign Off, p 110.

48. "Notes and Comment," New Yorker (Vol LVI, No 15, 2 June 1980), p 32.

49. McManus, Free At Last, p 51.

50. Sciolino, telephone conversation with the author.

51. Carter, Keeping Faith, p 503.

52. McManus, Free At Last!, p 91.

53. Robert D. McFadden, Joseph B. Treaster, and Maurice Caroll, No Hiding Place (New York: Times Books, 1981), p 71.

Conclusion

In both the United States and the United Kingdom, differences of opinion and intention arise between government and the press. No institution which is jealous of its own power, however deeply it may be committed to the philosophical ideal of a free press, can countenance constant scrutiny and frequent criticism without making some effort to protect itself. But the form of protection adopted by the state is markedly dissimilar in Britain and the United States.

In Britain this protection takes the form of restrictive legislation and negative official attitudes, which combine to place the press at a disadvantage in its relationship with government. Thus during the Falklands war it was common practice for government to withhold information point-blank from reporters both with the task force and in London. British refusal to permit a normal flow of information aboard task force ships, to admit the failure of the Port Stanley bombing raids, to announce the casualty tolls of HMS Galahad, and to reveal news of the Argentine surrender until after its announcement in the House of Commons — all these are examples of a type of behavior toward the press which exists in peacetime as in war. Conversely, government requests that journalists voluntarily withhold news occurred so rarely as to constitute a fluke in the normal pattern of behavior. In Britain, the press is not regarded as a powerful institution whose cooperation must be solicited. By the same token, the praise lavished by Thatcher and other officials on absurdly jingoistic tabloids like the Sun suggests that in Britain the government's respect for the press is so minimal as to permit honest expressions of enthusiasm about manifestly ludicrous newspapers.

In America the press enjoys a liberty which is institutionalized by legislation and supported — though not always willingly — by the attitude of government officials. Consequently, the state cannot afford to be high-handed in protecting itself from scrutiny. In the United States, therefore, government relies on two roundabout tactics: the appeal to journalistic self-restraint and the deliberate manipulation of the news. The Iranian hostage crisis witnessed few instances of direct suppression of information but numerous government attempts to manage the news and to induce self-restraint by the press. The secrecy surrounding the rescue mission was emphasized subsequently precisely because such secrecy occurred so rarely. On the other hand, instances of news management — like efforts to downplay the crisis after the rescue mission failed — abound, as do examples of attempts to impel self-restraint among journalists.

Not surprisingly, the press in Britain and the United States react differently to their dissimilar treatment at the hands of government. American journalists are so supremely self-confident of their importance to society that they are willing to exercise self-restraint in the interests of national security. However, they are unwilling to accept government definitions of national security, as coverage of the Iranian hostage crisis indicates. During the 1979–81 period the press responded selectively to official attempts to induce journalists self-restraint: the Washington Post agreed not to publish news of the Administration's secret negotiations with lawyers representing Iran, but Newsweek — which is owned and managed by the same organization — refused to withhold the names and photographs of the 50 hostages.

English journalists, by contrast, despair of gaining the respect and confidence of state officials. Consequently, they monitor their own professional behavior only to the extent necessary to avoid being called down for some infraction of the various laws that serve to check the press. Coverage of the Falklands war — the headline screaming "GOTCHA!" and the editorials proclaiming "We are all Falklanders now," as well as the less spectacular but equally shoddy reportage on the sweethearts, ambitions and life stories of innumerable task force soldiers — indicates the potential for mediocrity of a press denied information and accustomed to being held in poor repute.

If the emptiness of newspaper coverage in Britain is caused by the unwillingness of the state to regard the press as a locus of power with significant rights and privileges, then the lurid style which strives to disguise this emptiness is born of intense economic competition. The need to vie for readers and advertisers with seven rival newspapers has forced each daily national title into its own tight niche whose boundaries are defined in terms of editorial stance and audience social class. Such rarification of appeal has not ensured freedom from competition, however, and each newspaper in search of economic security seeks further guarantees of success in rampant sensationalism, as the inflammatory headlines, editorials and news coverage of the Falklands war proved only too clearly.

In the United States, by contrast, neither lack of access to news nor economic competition forces the press to adopt the irresponsible sensationalism of its British counterpart. American newspapers are secure in their ability to glean information from government officials and to survive economically by appealing exclusively to a precise geographic locality. Consequently, during the Iranian hostage crisis intensive press coverage and unusual patriotism among journalists did not degenerate into crass melodrama of the type witnessed in Britain during the Falklands war.

This difference of reportorial style in Britain and the United States is clearly manifested in coverage of official activities. The English press — leery of restrictive legislation and accustomed to a relatively insignificant role — tempers its sensationalism with extreme caution in reporting on the government. During the Falklands war, journalists were denied information and censored when they acquired it on their own initiative, but still they registered wholehearted support for the Thatcher government. Even the Guardian and the Daily Mirror, which both opposed the war, refrained for the most part from direct attack on individual officials and policies.

The American press, by contrast, is sufficiently secure in its position of legal freedom and official respect to criticize the government roundly. During the Iranian hostage crisis, the presence of reporters in Tehran was welcomed by the Carter Administration as an opportunity to communicate indirectly with a hostile nation, and journalists in Washington had access to virtually every bit of news received and every policy initiated by the United States. Nevertheless, at no time did the press support the Carter Administration with the unquestioning approbation shown by British newspapers for the Thatcher Government during the Falklands war.

The combination of legal restrictions, government disrespect and journalistic caution which characterizes the press in Britain does not bode well for the future. Regularly denied access to information and forced by economic exigencies to resort to crass sensationalism, British newspapers are ripe for co-optation by a Conservative Government which recognizes their potential for participation in a pro-Establishment coalition. For their part, Labour Governments ensure freedom of the press not because of any fundamental allegiance to the principle — disrespect for the press in Britain is endemic and therefore independent of party membership and political beliefs — but because they have no inherent affinity for a national press which is biased heavily in favor of the Right. Conservative Governments, on the other hand, could benefit mightily from mutually supportive relations with a national system of newspapers which favors the Right and would sooner guarantee its own economic success than uphold high standards or the principle of objectivity in reporting. If ever a Conservative Government sheds its traditional preconceptions concerning the press, therefore, freedom of the press in Britain may be profoundly endangered.

In the United States, on the other hand, the press is legally unfettered, journalists comment and criticize boldly, and government knows its place. Despite the ability of the Reagan Administration to score against the media throughout its six years in office, most spectacularly during the American invasion of Grenada, freedom of the press in the United States is supported by too many traditions to evaporate overnight. The most obvious of these are the First Amendment and the Freedom of Information Act. In addition to these legislative safeguards, the media are protected by several fundamental American attitudes. Tom Wicker maintains that "the public in this country is suspicious of too great a concentration of power." A national press whose might and influence rival those of the state risks incurring the kind of distrust and hostility that citizens usually reserve for government. However, if the media are fettered too severely by the state, Wicker avers, public opinion will shift in favor of the embattled press.

Yet another hidden factor operating in favor of the press is the habitual American distaste for secrecy. In the New York Times of 2 November 1983, James Reston characterized the United States as "a very gabby country. Nobody can make the American people shut up, or interfere with their freedom." (p A35) In his Times column of 18 January 1984, Anthony Lewis concurred, stating that "Leaks offend the tidy mind, but they happen to be the way business has been conducted in Washington for generations."

Appendixes

Date	Military	Political
April 1982		
2	Argentine invasion of Falklands; Royal Marines surrender.	British cabinet approves sending task force to South Atlantic.
3		First House of Commons sitting since Suez crisis (1956). UN passes Resolution 502 demanding Argentine withdrawal, an end to hostilities, and settlement by peaceful means.
5	First task force ships sail from Portsmouth.	Lord Carrington resigns as Foreign Secretary; Mr. Francis Pym takes his place.
7	Britain declares 200-mile military exclusion zone around Falklands.	Reagan approves Haig peace mission.
8		Haig negotiating team arrives in London.
9	HMS Canberra sails from Southampton.	EEC approves economic sanctions against Argentina.
10		Haig arrives in Buenos Aires.
12	Military exclusion zone comes into effect around Falklands.	Haig returns to London.
14	Argentine fleet embarks.	Haig returns to Washington to brief Reagan; Argentina appeals to UN.

April

15	British destroyers take up holding position in South Atlantic.	
17		Haig presents Argentina with peace plan.
19	South Georgia operation begins.	
22		Pym flies to Washington with British response to Haig peace proposals.
23		Foreign Office advises British in Argentina to leave.
25	South Georgia recaptured by British.	
27		Haig's final peace plan transmitted to London.
29	Task force arrives at military exclusion zone.	
30	Total military exclusion zone comes into force.	Reagan declares US support for British.

May

1	Initial British landings on Falklands. First raid on Port Stanley.	Pym returns to Washington.
2	Argentine carrier General Belgrano sunk.	Pym in New York. Peruvian and UN peace bids open.
3	Argentine patrol boats attacked.	Argentina rejects Peruvian peace proposal.

May

4	British destroyer HMS Sheffield sunk.	
5		British cabinet approves Peruvian peace plan.
6	Two British Harriers crash in fog.	Argentina rejects Peruvian peace plan again.
7	Military exclusion zone extended to 12 miles off Argentine coast.	Peace talks begin at UN.
11	QE2 leaves Southampton.	Argentina concedes sovereignty of Falklands not a precondition of peace.
15	British attack on Pebble Beach.	British delegates to UN return to London.
16		British cabinet draws up final proposals for UN. Delegates return to New York. EEC renews sanctions against Argentina.
18		Argentina rejects British proposals.
20		Thatcher tells House of Commons of collapse of peace proposals.
21	San Carlos landing; HMS Ardent sunk.	Open debate commences at Security Council.
23	HMS Antelope sunk. Seven Argentine aircraft lost.	
25	HMS Coventry and HMS Atlantic Conveyor lost.	

May

26		British cabinet questions lack of movement out of San Carlos. UN Resolution 505 bids UN President to seek settlement.
27	Movement out of San Carlos begins.	
28	British forces take Darwin and Goose Green.	
29	British bombard Argentine positions.	

June

1		British cabinet debates peace proposals made by Foreign Office and US.
2	British forces move to Bluff Cove. British troops take Mount Kent.	Argentine envoys arrive at UN and express willingness to surrender.
3		Versailles summit opens; Reagan's peace plan given to Britain.
4		Britain vetoes ceasefire resolution in Security Council.
6		Versailles summit supports British position.
8	HMS Galahad and HMS Tristram bombed.	British cabinet asked not to reveal casualties connected with HMS Galahad and HMS Tristram.
11	Battle of Port Stanley.	
14	Argentina surrenders.	

CHRONOLOGY: IRANIAN HOSTAGE CRISIS

<u>1979</u>

November 4:   Iranian militants seize the US Embassy in
               Tehran and take hostages. They demand
               that the US return the deposed Shah of Iran,
               Mohammed Rehza Pahlevi, who is in New
               York Hospital.

November 5:   The US rejects Iranian demands for the
               Shah's extradition.

November 7:   US authorizes former Attorney General Ram-
               sey Clark, a supporter of the Iranian revolu-
               tion, to travel to Iran and negotiate for the
               release of the hostages. Clark's efforts are
               rebuffed by Iran.

November 12:   US halts all oil imports from Iran.

November 14:   US freezes all official Iranian assets in
               American banks.

November 19:   Three of 13 Black and female hostages are
               freed.

November 20:   Remaining 10 Black and female hostages are
               freed. US moves naval task force to Indian
               Ocean and threatens to use force to free
               hostages.

November 25:   UN Security Council becomes involved in ne-
               gotiations to free hostages.

November 28:   Moderate Bani-Sadr is replaced as Foreign
               Minister by Sadegh Ghotbzadeh, who advo-
               cates releasing the hostages only after the
               extradition of the Shah.

November 29:   US files suit against Iran in the International
               Court of Justice.

December 2:   US decides to provide sanctuary for the Shah
               after Mexico refuses to readmit him follow-
               ing his operation in the US.

December 10:	NBC airs controversial interview with hostage Marine Corporal William Gallegos.
December 12:	US expels Iranian diplomats.
December 15:	Shah leaves US for Panama.
December 25:	Hostages celebrate Christmas with visiting Western clergymen.

1980

January 1:	US Security General Kurt Waldheim arrives in Iran to attempt to expedite the release of the hostages.
January 4:	After failing to meet with Khomeini and encountering hostility, Waldheim departs Iran.
January 14:	Iranian Revolutionary Council expels US journalists.
January 29:	Six American officials escape Iran (not from embassy) by posing as Canadian businessmen.
February 4:	Bani-Sadr becomes President of Iran.
February 19:	Iran formally accepts the offer of a five-member commission, headed by Waldheim, to investigate Iranian charges against the Shah and the US.
March 11:	Waldheim commission leaves Iran after meeting with hostility and non-cooperation.
March 23:	Shah leaves Panama for Egypt.
April 1:	Bani-Sadr offers to take custody of hostages if Carter ceases to criticize Iran and lifts economic and diplomatic sanctions; Carter accepts the offer.
April 7:	Khomeini overrules Bani-Sadr's offer and rules that hostages must remain in custody of militants. US breaks diplomatic relations with Iran.

April	18:	US imposes new economic sanctions against Iran and warns of impending military action.
April	24:	Rescue mission to free hostages fails.
April	28:	Secretary of State Cyrus Vance resigns over rescue mission.
May	18:	EEC imposes limited economic sanctions against Iran.
June	2:	Defying a US ban on civilian travel to Iran, Ramsey Clark and nine others fly to Iran to participate in investigation of Iranian grievances against US.
June	10:	Carter announces desire to prosecute Clark for disobedience of injunction against travel to Iran.
July	10:	Hostage Richard Queen is freed because of illness. (He is later diagnosed as having multiple sclerosis.)
July	27:	Shah dies in Egypt.
Sept	12:	Khomeini lists four conditions for hostages' release — return of the Shah's wealth, cancellation of US claims against Iran, unfreezing of Iranian funds in US, and US guarantees not to interfere in Iranian affairs — but, significantly, omits earlier demand for US apology.
Sept	19:	Fighting breaks out between Iran and Iraq.
October	29:	US promises Iran $220 million in military equipment for ongoing war with Iraq if hostages are freed.
Nov	3:	Algeria agrees to mediate negotiations between US and Iran.
Nov	20:	US accepts four Iranian conditions in principle.

Nov   27:   Militants cede custody of hostages to Iranian government.

Dec   21:   Iran demands that US turn over $24 billion in cash and gold (equivalent to Iranian estimate of the Shah's wealth and Iranian frozen assets) before the hostages are freed; US denounces this demand as unreasonable.

1981

January 10:   US tells Iran that Iranian funds in US would be unfrozen within several days of hostages' release.

January 18:   US and Iran agree on terms for release of hostages.

January 20:   Hostages are released.

Bibliography

PRIMARY SOURCES

<u>Personal Communications with the Author</u>

Auerbach, Stuart, <u>Washington Post</u>, Washington DC. Telephone conversation, 14 December 1983.

Barnett, Anthony, <u>New Left Review</u>, London, England. Letter, December 1983.

Brzezinski, Zbigniew, Center for Strategic and International Studies, Washington DC. Telephone conversation, 16 December 1983.

Cody, Edward, <u>Washington Post</u>, Washington DC. Letter, December 1983.

Gergen, David, Kennedy School of Government (Harvard University), Cambridge MA. Interview, 7 March 1984.

Holden, Anthony, <u>Daily Express</u>, London, England. Interview, 10 September 1983.

Ingham, Bernard, Press Office of the Prime Minister, London, England. Interview, 9 September 1983.

James, Henry, National Association of Pension Funds, London, England. Interview, 7 September 1983.

McDonald, Ian, Ministry of Defence, London, England. Interview, 6 September 1983.

94

Middleton, Drew, New York Times, New York City. Interview, 3 November 1983; and telephone conversation, 17 November 1983.

Nott, John, Lazard Brothers, England. Interview, 6 September 1983.

Powell, Jody, Powell and Associates, Washington DC. Interview, 21 December 1983.

Reston, James, New York Times, New York City. Telephone conversation, 17 November 1983.

Saunders, Harold, American Enterprise Institute, Washington DC. Interview, 21 December 1983.

Sciolino, Elaine, Newsweek, New York City. Telephone conversation, 12 November 1983.

Underwood, John, Independent Television News, London, England. Interview, 6 September 1983.

Vance, Cyrus, Simpson Thacher and Bartlett, New York City. Interview, 15 December 1983.

Wicker, Tom, New York Times, New York City. Interview, 15 December 1983.

Witherow, John, The Times, London, England. Interview, 8 September 1983.

Miscellaneous

Archer, Geoffrey, "Evidence to the Defence Committee," Letter written July 1982.

BBC Information Division, "The Falklands Conflict — and the war of words over the BBC's coverage." Newspaper articles compiled Summer, 1982.

"Falkland Sound/Voces de Malvinas," at the Royal Theatre, Summer, 1983.

Great Britain, Defence Committee of the House of Commons, "The Handling of Press and Public Information During the Falklands Conflict," Volume I. Report, 8 December 1982.

Great Britain, Committee of Privy Counsellors, "Falkland Island Review." Report, January 1983.

Great Britain, Office of the Secretary of State for Defence,"The Falklands Campaign: The Lessons." Report, December 1982.

Ingham, Bernard, Lecture presented at the conference of the Guild of British Newspaper Editors, Cardiff, Wales, May 1983.

Mashek, John, US News and World Report, Washington DC. Lecture delivered at Harvard University, 16 November 1983.

Page, Susan, Newsday, Long Island NY. Lecture delivered at Harvard University, 30 November 1983.

Simons, Richard, and Green, Michael, Memorandum to David Nicholas, Independent Television News, London, England, July 1983.

United States Department of Defense, Current News Special Edition: The Press in Grenada, No 115, 22 February 1984.

Newspapers Monitored

Daily Mirror (London), March–June 1982.

Guardian (London), March–June 1982.

New York Times, November 1979–January 1981, November 1983–February 1984.

Sun (London), March–June 1982.

The Times (London), March–June 1982.

Washington Post, November 1979–January 1981.

SECONDARY SOURCES

Books

Assersohn, Roy, The Biggest Deal. London: Methuen London Ltd., 1982.

Bagdikian, Ben, The Effete Conspiracy. New York: Harper and Row, 1972.

_____, The Information Machines. New York: Harper and Row, 1971.

_____, The Media Monopoly. Boston: Beacon Press, 1983.

Balk, Alfred, A Free and Responsive Press. New York: The Twentieth Century Fund, 1973.

Barnett, Anthony, Iron Britannia. London: Allison and Busby, 1982.

Bishop, Patrick and Witherow, John, The Winter War. London: Quartet Books, 1982.

Brown, Charlene J., Brown, Trevor R. and Rivers, William L., The Media and the People. New York: Holt, Rinehart and Winston, 1978.

Brzezinski, Zbigniew, Power and Principle. New York: Farrar Straus Giroux, 1983.

Cannon, Lou, Reporting: An Inside View. USA: Lou Cannon, 1977.

Carlsen, Robin Woodsworth, Crisis In Iran. Canada: The Snow Man Press, 1979.

Carter, Jimmy, Keeping Faith. New York: Bantam Books, 1982.

Cater, Douglass, The Fourth Branch of Government. Boston: Houghton Mifflin Company, 1959.

Cohen, Bernard C., The Press and Foreign Policy. Princeton NJ: Princeton University Press, 1963.

Curran, James, ed., <u>The British Press: A Manifesto</u>. London: The MacMillan Press Ltd., 1978.

Deakin, James, <u>Straight Stuff: The Reporters, The White House and the Truth</u>. New York: William Morrow, 1984.

Diamond, Edwin, <u>Sign Off</u>. Cambridge MA: The MIT Press, 1982.

Dobson, Christopher, Miller, John and Payne, Ronald, <u>The Falklands Conflict</u>. London: Coronet Books, 1982.

Dorsen, Norman and Gillers, Stephen, eds., <u>None of Your Business</u>. New York: The Viking Press, 1974.

Dunn, Delmar D., <u>Public Officials and the Press</u>. Reading MA: Addison-Wesley Publishing Company, 1969.

Emery, Edwin, <u>The Press and America</u>. Englewood Cliffs NJ: Prentice-Hall, Inc., 1972.

Evans, Harold, <u>Good Times, Bad Times</u>. New York: Atheneum, 1984.

Grundy, Bill, <u>The Press Inside Out</u>. London: W.H. Allen, 1976.

Hanrahan, Brian, and Fox, Robert, <u>I Counted Them All Out and I Counted Them All Back</u>. London: British Broadcasting Corporation, 1982.

Harris, Robert, <u>Gotcha! The Media, the Government and the Falklands Crisis</u>. Boston: Faber and Faber, Inc., 1983.

Hastings, Max and Jenkins, Simon, <u>The Battle for the Falklands</u>. London: Michael Joseph, 1983.

Heise, Juergen Arthur, <u>Minimum Disclosure: How The Pentagon Manipulates the News</u>. New York: W.W. Norton and Company, 1979.

Henry, Harry, <u>Behind the Headlines — the Business of the British Press</u>. London: Associated Business Press, 1978.

Hiebert, Ray Eldon, ed., <u>The Press In Washington</u>. New York: Dodd, Mead and Company, 1966.

Hirsch, Fred and Gordon, David, Newspaper Money. London: Hutchinson & Co., Ltd., 1975.

Jenkins, Simon, Newspapers. London: Faber and Faber, 1979.

Johnson, Haynes, In the Absence of Power. New York: The Viking Press, 1982.

Jordan, Hamilton, Crisis: The Last Year of the Carter Presidency. New York: G.P. Putnam's Sons, 1982.

Knightley, Phillip, The First Casualty. New York: Harcourt Brace Jovanovich, 1975.

Koob, Kathryn, Guest of the Revolution. New York: Thomas Nelson Publishers, 1982.

McFadden, Robert D., Treaster, Joseph B., and Carroll, Maurice, No Hiding Place. New York: Times Books, 1981.

McManus, Doyle, Free At Last! New York: The New American Library, Inc., 1981.

Merrill, John C. and Fisker, Harold A., The World's Great Dailies: Profiles of Fifty Newspapers. New York: Hasting House, 1980.

Powell, Jody, The Other Side of the Story. New York: William Morrow, 1984.

Queen, Richard, Inside and Out. New York: G.P. Putnam's Sons, 1981.

Reston, James, The Artillery of the Press. New York: Harper and Row, 1966.

Rivers, William L., The Other Government. New York: Universe Books, 1982.

Rubin, Barry, Paved with Good Intentions. New York: Oxford University Press, 1980.

Salinger, Pierre, America Held Hostage: The Secret Negotiations. Garden City, NY: Doubleday and Company, Inc., 1981.

Siebert, Fred S., Peterson, Theodore, and Schramm, Wilbur, Four Theories of the Press. Freeport NY: Books for Libraries Press, 1956.

Sigal, Leon V., Reporters and Officials: The Organization and Politics of Newsmaking. Lexington MA: D.C. Heath and Company, 1973.

Smith, Anthony, Goodbye Gutenberg: The Newspaper Revolution of the 1980's. New York: Oxford University Press, 1980.

Sunday Express Magazine Team, War in the Falklands. London: Weidenfeld and Nicolson, 1982.

Sunday Times Insight Team, The Falklands War. London: Sphere Books Limited, 1982.

Vance, Cyrus, Hard Choices. New York: Simon and Schuster, 1983.

Whale, John, The Politics of the Media. Manchester: Manchester University Press, 1977.

Wicker, Tom, On Press. New York: The Viking Press, 1978.

Wintour, Charles, Pressures on the Press. London: Andre Deutsch Limited, 1972.

Woolf, Cecil and Wilson, Jean Moorcroft, Authors Take Sides on the Falklands. London: Cecil Woolf Publishers, 1982.

Unpublished Materials

Ecoropa Information Sheet #11, "Falklands War: The Disturbing Truth," pamphlet printed at Caerphilly by P.G. Printing, 1982.

Glasgow Media Group, "War and Peace." Report issued by the Department of Sociology, University of Glasgow, 1982.

James, Henry, "Public Relations in Conflict: The Lesson of the Falklands." Newsletter of the Institute of Public Relations, July 1983.

Parmelee, Jennifer, "From Firemen to Diplomats: The Western Media and Iran Before and After the Revolution." Near Eastern Studies Senior Thesis, Princeton University, 6 May 1980.

Raphel, Arnold, "Media Coverage of the Hostage Negotiations — From Fact to Fiction." Unpublished paper presented for the Twenty-Fourth Session of the US Department of State (Foreign Service Institute) Executive Seminar in National and International Affairs, February 1982.

Magazine/Newspaper Articles

Adler, Jerry, "In War, Truth or Faction?" Newsweek, Vol XCIX, No 21, 24 May 1982, p 86.

America, editorial, V-1 146, No 21, 29 May 1982, p 412.

Barnett, Anthony, "Getting It Wrong and Making It Right," New Socialist, No 13, September/October 1983, pp 44–47.

Beloff, Nora, "Last Chance for British Newspapers: Has Fleet Street A Chance?" Encounter, Vol XLIX, No 3, September 1977, pp 82–88.

Bingham, Worth and Just, Ward S., "The President and the Press." Reporter, Vol 26, No 8, 12 April 1962, pp 18–22.

Cater, Douglass and Bartlett, Charles L., "Is All the News Fit to Print?" Reporter, Vol 24, No 10, 11 May 1961, pp 23–24.

_____, "News and the Nation's Security." Reporter, Vol 25, No 1, 6 July 1961, pp 26–29.

Clark, Ramsey, "The Iranian Solution," Nation, Vol 230, No 24, 21 June 1980, pp 3–5.

Clarke, Gerald, "Covering an Uncoverable War," Time, Vol 119, No 20, 17 May 1982, p 53.

Cockburn, Alexander, "Fact Shortage No Problem, Analysts Say." Harpers, Vol 265, No 1586, July 1982, pp 27–31.

Dorman, William A. and Omeed, Ensan, "Reporting Iran the Shah's Way," Columbia Journalism Review, Vol 17, No 5, January/February 1979, pp 27–33.

Fairlie, Henry, "Hostages of Television," New Republic, Vol 184, No 6, 7 January 1981, pp 9–11.

"Foreign Encounter," Nation, Vol 230, No 23, 14 June 1980, p 1.

Henry, William A. III, "Journalism Under Fire," Time, Vol 122, No 25, 12 December 1983, pp 76–93.

Holden, Anthony, "Fleet Street's War," New Republic, Vol 187, 5 July 1982, p 17.

Hurewitz, J.C., "Another View on Iran and the Press," Columbia Journalism Review, Vol XIX, No 1, May/June 1980, pp 19–21.
Kaiser, Charles, "Behind 'Enemy' Lines," Newsweek, Vol XCIX, No 17, 26 April 1982, p 57.

Langdon, Julia, "The War at the Ballot Box," Macleans, Vol 95, No 20, 17 May 1982, p 21.

Leo, John, "A War Ever Tougher to Cover," Time, Vol 119, No 21, 24 May 1982, p 70.

Levin, Bob, "A Lift for the Tories," Newsweek, Vol XCIX, No 24, 14 June 1982, p 57.

"Lost Chance?", Nation, Vol 230, No 3, 26 January 1980, pp 67–68.

NBC, "20/20" and "Nightline," 22 January 1981. "America Held Hostage: The Secret Negotiations," narrated by Pierre Salinger.

Neier, Aryeh, "Right to Travel," Nation, Vol 230, No 17, 3 May 1980, p 1.

"Notes and Comment," New Yorker, Vol LVI, No 11, 5 May 1980, pp 31–32.

"Notes and Comment," New Yorker, Vol LVI, No 12, 12 May 1980, pp 31–32.

"Notes and Comment," New Yorker, Vol LVI, No 15, 2 June 1980, pp 31–32.

Panter–Downes, Mollie, "Letter From London," New Yorker, Vol LVIII, No 15, 31 May 1982, p 91.

Peer, Elizabeth, "The Story of a Lifetime," Newsweek, Vol XCVII, No 5, 2 February 1981, pp 76–77.

Said, Edward W., "Hiding Islam," Harpers, Vol 262, No 1568, January 1981, pp 25–32.

von Hoffman, Nicholas, "ABC Held Hostage," New Republic, Vol 182, No 19, 10 May 1980, pp 15–17.

Wall, James M., "Editorial Comment: 'Dog Day Afternoon' Revisited," Christian Century, Vol XCVII, No 15, 23 April 1980, pp 459–460.

Magazines Monitored

Economist, March–June 1982

Editor and Publisher, November 1983–February 1984

Newsweek, November 1979–January 1981

Time, November 1979–January 1981, November 1983–February 1984

Index

Advertising revenues, 2, 3,
    4, 5, 16
Albala, Nuri, 57
Allison, Graham, 68
Antarctic, 22, 25
Anti-defamation laws, 5
Argentina, 21-22. See also
    Falklands conflict
Army (British), 23, 27, 30
Artillery of the Press, The
    (Reston), 5
Auerbach, Stuart, 54, 55
Authoritarian states press, 1
Azerbaijani minorities (Iran),
    55

Background information, 14
Bakhtiar, Shahpur, 53
Bani-Sadr, Abolhassan, 56,
    66, 70, 74
Barnett, Anthony, 33
BBC. See British Broadcasting
    Corporation
Beards, 55
Belgrano (Argentine cruiser),
    38, 39
Bishop, Patrick, 27
Bourget (lawyer), 56, 62
British Broadcasting Corpo-
    ration (BBC), 31, 36-37,
    41, 44
  World Service, 30

British press
  censorship, 2, 28-30, 32-37,
    83
  and class differences, 3,
    4-5, 16, 83
  and competition, 2, 3, 4-5,
    16, 38, 42-43, 44, 83
  conservative, 4, 5, 16, 38,
    84
  daily, 38, 42
  and Falklands conflict, 22-
    44, 51, 81, 82, 83
  as free, 2, 5, 15, 84
  and government intervention,
    1, 2, 6, 8, 9, 15, 81, 82,
    83-84. See also Official
    Secrets Act
  and government relations,
    10-11, 15-16, 21, 22-44,
    81, 82-83
  image of, 10, 44, 81, 84
  left-wing. See Guardian
  national organization of, 3
  opinion polls, 42
  and Parliamentary debates,
    9
  revenues, 3, 4
  sensationalism, 16, 26, 82,
    83, 84
  and standardizing editorial
    policies, 3, 4
  Sunday, 38

103

conflict
Greenfield, Meg, 71, 72
Grenada, 84
Guardian (London), 37, 38, 39,
    42, 83

Hastings, Max, 26, 30
Holden, Anthony, 10, 32, 41
House of Commons (Great
    Britain), 11, 22, 30, 36,
    81
  Defence Committee, 25, 28,
    29, 32, 33, 34

Independent Television News
    (ITN), 2, 22, 26, 29, 32,
    33
Information leakage, 30-31,
    57, 84
Ingham, Bernard, 24, 35, 36
Iran, 55
  hostage crisis chronology,
    89-92
  revolution (1978), 52-53
  See also United States press,
    and Iranian hostage crisis
ITN. See Independent Tele-
    vision News

James, Henry, 8, 24, 25, 26,
    31, 32, 34
JIC. See Joint Intelligence
    Committee
Jingoism, 26, 38-42, 43
Joint Intelligence Committee
    (JIC) (Great Britain), 22
Jordan, Hamilton, 62

Kennedy, Edward, 57
Khomeini, Ruhollah (ayatollah),
    55, 56, 57, 65, 66, 70, 71
Kraft, Joseph, 66
Kurdish minorities (Iran), 55

Labour Party (Great Britain),
    4, 22, 39, 41, 84
Lewis, Anthony, 61, 65, 84

Los Angeles Times, 74

MacBride, Sean, 57
McDonald, Ian, 23, 31, 32, 34,
    36, 43
McManus, Doyle, 74
"MacNeil-Lehrer Report," 54
MacQueen, Alistair, 29
Magazines, 2
Marines (British), 35
Mediator, 74-75
Members of Parliament (MPs),
    11, 36
Middleton, Drew, 75
Military communications
    systems, 27-28
Mirage aircraft, 35
Mirror. See Daily Mirror
Misinformation, 33, 56
MoD. See Defence, Ministry of
Monopolies, 4
MPs. See Members of Parlia-
    ment
Murdoch, Rupert, 4, 22, 39

Nation (magazine), 62
National Broadcasting Company
    (NBC), 63
National Front (Iran), 53
Nationalism, 51, 71-75
National Publishers' Associa-
    tion (NPA) (Great Britain),
    23
National Security Agency
    (U.S.), 9
National Security Council
    (U.S.), 53
Navy
  British, 23, 25, 27-28, 29,
    35
  U.S., 65
NBC. See National Broad-
    casting Company
Neckties, 55
Newsday (Long Island, N.Y.),
    14, 58, 64
News management, 14-15, 56,

WIDENER UNIVERSITY
WOLFGRAM
LIBRARY
CHESTER, PA.